ASSEMBLY OF MASORTI SYNAGOGUES
1097 FINCHLEY ROAD
LONDON NW11 0PU
TEL: 0181 201 8772 FAX: 0181 201 8917

It is often supposed that Judaism is a group-centred religion which places little emphasis on the individual. Dr Jacobs here demonstrates that such a view is fallacious. He admits that, as is the case with other religious traditions, there are tensions in Judaism between the community of believers as a whole and the individual worshipper. However, through a careful analysis of primary texts, he shows that the role of the individual is a significant one in Judaism, and that in most versions of the faith the ultimate aim of the individual is to inherit eternal life.

RELIGION AND THE INDIVIDUAL
A JEWISH PERSPECTIVE

CAMBRIDGE STUDIES IN RELIGIOUS TRADITIONS

Edited by John Clayton (University of Lancaster), Steven Collins (University of Chicago) and Nicholas de Lange (University of Cambridge)

1. *Religion and the individual: a Jewish perspective*
   Louis Jacobs
2. *The body divine: the symbol of the body in the works of Teilhard de Chardin and Rāmānuja*
   Anne Hunt Overzee

RELIGION AND THE INDIVIDUAL

A Jewish perspective

LOUIS JACOBS

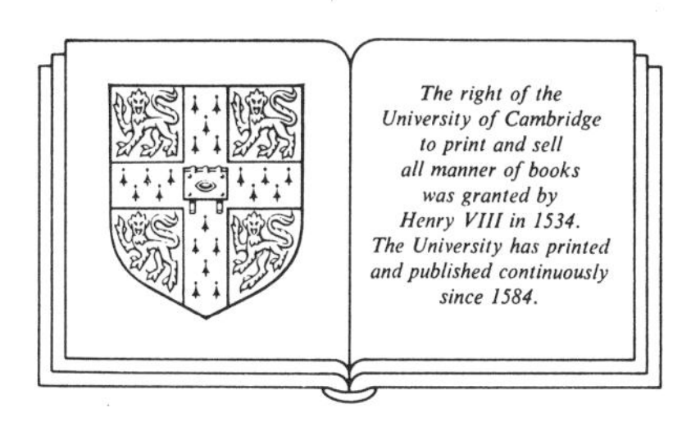

CAMBRIDGE UNIVERSITY PRESS

Cambridge
New York Port Chester
Melbourne Sidney

Published by the Press Syndicate of the University of Cambridge
The Pitt Building, Trumpington Street, Cambridge CB2 1RP
40 West 20th Street, New York, NY 10011–4211, USA
10 Stamford Road, Oakleigh, Victoria 3166, Australia

First published 1992

Printed in Great Britain at the University Press, Cambridge

A cataloguing in publication record for this book is available from the British Library

Library of Congress cataloguing in publication data

Jacobs, Louis,
Religion and the individual: a Jewish perspective / Louis Jacobs.
p. cm. – (Cambridge Studies in Religious Traditions; 1)
Includes bibliographical references and index.
ISBN 0 521 41138 6 (hardback)
1. Man (Jewish theology) 2. Individualism–Religious aspects – Judaism. 3. Judaism–Doctrines. I. Title. II. Series.
BM627.J34 1991
296.322–dc20 91 – 8138 CIP

ISBN 0 521 41138 6 HARDBACK

UP

For Shula: my individualist and my love

Contents

Preface

This book is a study of the role of the individual in religion from the perspective of Judaism. The book has been written in the conviction that both apologists for Judaism and hostile critics have erred in relegating the individual to a less than central place. Most of the material is presented here for the first time except for chapters 7 and 10. An earlier version of chapter 7 appeared in *Studies in Rationalism, Judaism and Universalism in Memory of Leon Roth*, ed. Raphael Loewe, London, 1966 ('The Doctrine of the "Divine Spark" in Man in Jewish Sources', pp. 87–114) and of chapter 10 in the journal *Conservative Judaism*, 34, September / October, 1980 ('Divine Foreknowledge and Human Free Will', pp. 4–16), for which my thanks are due to the editors. Although, nowadays, especially in the United States, various circumlocutions would be used in writing about the individual so as to avoid the taint of male chauvinism, I find such forms as he/she to be quite unnecessary even in a work about the individual. The individual is referred to in this book in the male form purely out of convention and to avoid an awkward English style.

Abbreviations

ARN	*Avot de-Rabbi Nathan*
b.	ben, 'son of'
CCAR	Central Conference of American Rabbis
CE	Common Era
EJ	*Encyclopedia Judaica*
ERE	*Encyclopedia of Religion and Ethics*, ed. James Hastings
ET	*Entziklopedia Talmudit*
HUCA	*Hebrew Union College Annual*
JE	*Jewish Encyclopedia*
JJS	*Journal of Jewish Studies*
Maharam	Novellae of R Meir of Lublin (d. 1616)
Maharsha	Novellae of R Samuel Edels (1555–1631)
Meiri	*Bet ha-Beḥirah*, by Menahem Meiri of Perpignan (1249–1316)
R	Rabbi
Raabad	R Abraham Ibn David (d. 1198)
Radbaz	R David Ibn Abi Zimra (1479–1573)
Ramban	R Moses b. Nahman, Nahmanides (1194–1270)
Ran	R Nissim Gerondi (d. *c.* 1375)
Rashba	R Solomon Ibn Adret (*c.* 1235–*c.* 1310)
Rashi	R Solomon Yitzhaki (1040–1105)
Redak	R David Kimhi (1160–1235)
Ribash	R Isaac b. Sheshet Perfet (1326–1408)
Shelah	*Sheney Luḥot ha-Berit*, by Isaiah Horowitz (d. 1630)
Soncino	The Babylonian Talmud, translated into English, Soncino Press
Tur	The *Turim* of R Jacob b. Asher (d. 1430)
UJE	*Universal Jewish Encyclopedia*

CHAPTER I

Individual significance

It is a truism that Judaism is centred around the Jewish people. This is expressed in the very names for the religion: Judaism, derived from the Greek, and *torat yisrael* or *dat yisrael* in Hebrew. When called to the reading of the Torah, the Jew recites the benediction: 'Blessed art thou, O Lord our God, King of the universe, who has chosen us from all peoples, and hast given us thy Torah.' The Jewish festivals and fasts commemorate events, joyous or tragic, in the history of the people: the Exodus on Passover; the giving of the Torah on Shavuot; the dwelling in booths on Tabernacles; the deliverance from Antiochus on Hanukkah and from Haman's machinations on Purim; the breach of the walls of Jerusalem on the seventeenth of Tammuz and the destruction of the Temple on Tisha be-Av. Even on Rosh ha-Shanah, when the universalistic note is sounded, and on Yom Kippur, when individual remorse finds its strongest expression, the prayers are voiced in the plural form in such a way that it is the people of Israel who come to present themselves to God on these solemn occasions. Reform Judaism, too, is people-centred, with the Reform idea of the 'mission of Israel' to be 'a light unto the nations'. After the Holocaust and the establishment of the State of Israel, an even greater emphasis has naturally been placed on Jewish peoplehood.

This stress on the Jewish community has provided Jews with the fortitude to survive and it has freed the individual Jew from a morbid retreat into egotism and selfhood. Yet it cannot be denied that it has often resulted in a marked imbalance in which the needs of the individual Jew, both material and spiritual, tend to be relegated to the background of Jewish life, if not completely ignored, as, to give a contemporary instance, when some Rabbis urge their flock to have more children solely in order to make good the incredible losses by increasing the Jewish population.

The aim of this book is to demonstrate that, for all the admitted emphasis on peoplehood, there are equally powerful individualistic tendencies in Judaism it is perilous to overlook. In any balanced view of Judaism, what the individual does with his life has eternal significance for him, not only for the Jewish people, itself made up of individuals. It is only in totalitarian systems that the individual exists for the group rather than the group for the individuals of which it is comprised.

A good starting-point for an investigation of how Judaism views the significance of the individual is the oft-quoted statement in the Mishnah, tractate *Sanhedrin* 4:5. This passage in the Mishnah discusses the procedure to be adopted by the ancient Court of Law in warning the witnesses to a capital charge of the sacredness of human life. (It should be remarked that by the time the Mishnah was compiled, towards the end of the second century, the right of the Courts to inflict capital punishment had long been in abeyance, but the fact that the discussion is academic in no way renders it irrelevant to our inquiry.) A man is on trial for his life and though it is the duty of the witnesses to his crime to testify against him, if he is guilty, they must not embark on this without being fully conscious of the enormity of destroying an innocent life. As a reminder of the seriousness of what they are doing, the witnesses are to be referred, states the Mishnah, to the Genesis narrative of Adam and Eve, in which all mankind is descended from these two, ultimately from a single human being since Eve was formed from Adam's rib. This is how the Mishnah puts it:

> Therefore but a single man was at first created in the world, to teach that if anyone has caused a single person to perish Scripture imputes it to him as though he had caused a whole world to perish; and if anyone saves the life of a single person Scripture imputes it to him as though he had saved a whole world. Again [but a single man was created] for the sake of peace among mankind, that none should say to his fellow: 'My father was greater than your father' [since all have ultimately the same father, Adam]; also that the heretics should not say, 'There are many ruling powers' [each creating his own race of humans]. Again [but a single man was created], to proclaim the greatness of the Holy One, blessed is He; for when a man stamps many coins with the same seal they are all alike; but the Holy One, blessed be He, has stamped every human being with the seal of the first man, yet no two are exactly alike. Therefore, everyone is required to say, 'For my sake the world was created'.

It has been noted that, in the original texts of the Mishnah (in many current texts the word *yisrael* has been added without warrant) it is the significance of every human being that is affirmed, as is clear from the proof-text from the Adam narrative, the father of the whole human race. In polytheistic religion, the Mishnah implies, each god can have his favourite but in monotheism all human beings are ultimately of equal worth in terms of human dignity. Moreover, each individual, a potential progenitor of a whole world, is a world in himself and is entitled to see himself as the reason in himself for the creation of the whole world. He is not simply a minute fragment of the human race. He is the human race and whatever purposes God has for creating the human race are totally realized in him. There are, of course, billions of other members of the human race but each of these, too, is an end in himself, not only a means to a more glorious, because more embracing, end, that of humanity as the whole. The Mishnah also points to the fact that no two persons are exactly alike. (We now know that, for example, no two human beings have an identical set of fingerprints.) Each individual is a unique creation.

It is true that the Mishnah is not making any hard and fast, precise theological statement. Of these, there are very few indeed in the Talmudic literature, and there are, without doubt, Talmudic observations with a more pronounced group or community emphasis. For all that, after this Mishnah, it cannot be seriously maintained that Judaism ignores in any way the role of the individual.[1]

Working back from the Mishnah to the Bible and forward to the Talmud and the middle ages it is not at all difficult to see the role of the individual as a prominent theme throughout all the periods of Jewish history.

With regard to the Biblical period, the contention of some Old Testament scholars that all the stress was on the nation, until the later prophets taught individual responsibility,[2] must be rejected even on a superficial reading of the earlier sources. In the patriarchal narratives, for example, while it is now axiomatic that these often reflect tribal motifs,[3] yet each of the patriarchs and matriarchs appears as a person with the strongest individual characteristics. The pioneering Abraham is different from an Isaac who follows in his father's footsteps and both are different from a Jacob who relies on his grandfather's and father's teachings to build the 'house of Israel'.[4] Of the three leaders of the people through the forty years of wandering in the wilderness, Moses is the stern lawgiver, Aaron the priestly figure, bent on compromise for the sake of peace, while Miriam adopts the feminine role, watching over her infant brother and eventually leading all the women in singing her own song of deliverance at the shores of the sea.

Both the first paragraph of the Shema (Deuteronomy 6:4–9) and the Decalogue (Exodus 20:114; Deuteronomy 5:6–18) are in the singular and are addressed to each individual; the same is true of the majority of the laws in the three Pentateuchal Codes (Exodus 21:1 – 23:19; Leviticus 19:1–37; Deuteronomy 21:1 – 25:19).[5]

As for the prophets, each of these speaks as an individual, his communication from God expressed in terms of his own temperament and particular circumstances. And, while the prophetic message is generally to the people as a whole, the call of the prophets is for the individuals of that people to be governed by justice, righteousness, holiness and compassion. Ezekiel chapter 18 is a powerful plea for individual responsibility. Micah's famous declaration of what it is that God demands is in the singular and is addressed to each member of the group:

> It hath been told thee, O man,
> what is good,
> And what the Lord doth require
> of thee:
> Only to do justly, and to love
> mercy, and to walk humbly with
> thy God. (Micah. 6:8)

In the Talmudic and Midrashic literature, the emphasis is generally on peoplehood but statements regarding individual duties, responsibilities and needs are found throughout this literature. Each of the Rabbis is an individual with his own particular virtues and failings, so much so that it has been possible, with a fair degree of success, to reconstruct Rabbinic biographies from the hints scattered in this vast literature.[6] In the story of Hillel and the prospective proselyte,[7] Hillel states the golden rule in the singular: 'That which is hateful unto thee do not do unto thy neighbour.' In a typical passage in the Babylonian Talmud,[8] after the various rules for communal prayer have been stated (the statutory prayer, the *Tefillah*, is in the plural form and the same for all), a number of individual prayers are recorded, each of the Rabbis mentioned composing his own prayer in accordance with his particular circumstances. And over and above the numerous statements about the Torah for Gentiles in the form of the seven Noahide laws,[9] there are references to the Gentile as well as the Jew as an individual, as when a Rabbi said[10] that Scripture declares: 'Which if a man do, he shall live by them' (Leviticus 18:5). It does not say a priest or a Levite or an Israelite but a *man*, to teach that a Gentile who practises the Torah (i.e. follows the Noahide laws) is the equal of the High Priest. A late Midrash[11] is even more emphatic: 'I bring heaven and earth to witness that the Holy Spirit rests upon a Gentile as well as a Jew, upon a woman as well as a man, upon a maid-servant as well as a man-servant. All depends on the needs of the particular individual' (*le-fi ma'asav shel adam*).

In the philosophical tradition in the middle ages, especially in Maimonides,[12] Judaism is so interpreted that the aim of the religion is ultimately for the individual, the social thrust of Judaism being treated as a means to an end; a sound social order helps the individual to rise towards perfection. Maimonides' thirteen principles of the Jewish faith[13] are directed towards the individual Jew. It is no accident that Maimonides does not list the belief in Israel as the Chosen People among his thirteen principles. It is not that Maimonides does not believe that Israel has been chosen by God but that such a belief is not so prominent a feature of the Jewish religion that it can be designated a principle of the faith.[14]

In the Kabbalah, every human soul is a spark of Adam's soul, bound to engage in the task of restoration of the holy sparks that fell into the demonic realm when Adam sinned. In the Kabbalistic doctrine of *tikkun*, 'rectification', each individual has his own special role to play according to his particular soul-root.[15] In Hasidism the soul-root idea is developed still further. Not only does the *ḥasid* have to find the Zaddik whose personality is in accord with his particular soul (because they are of the same 'root') but there are fallen sparks in creation which only a particular individual can raise because these, too, belong to his soul-root.[16]

Of course, to rely solely on the above is to distort Judaism. The truth of the matter is that throughout all periods there has been considerable tension between peoplehood and individualism in Judaism as there has been between Jewish particularism and universalism. The aim of this chapter has been to note, especially, the individualistic trends. In the following chapters the inevitable qualifications to individualism will be examined. It will become clear, I hope, that there is no simple answer to the question: Does Judaism centre on the people or on the individual? It centres on both.

There is a further severe problem to be faced in this inquiry. The term 'individual' with its abstract connotation was unknown in the classical sources of Judaism and is foreign to their way of thinking. Except in purely numerical contexts, the individual is never seen in isolation from the group to which he belongs.

Take the Mishnah quoted above. Superficially, there can be no more cogent evidence of emphasis on the individual than the statements in the Mishnah that to save a single human life is to save a whole world and that one is obliged to say: For my sake the world was created. And yet in both statements the individual is not given a completely autonomous status. The life of the individual is indeed declared to be of supreme significance but only in the context of the whole world. To save a single human life is to save a 'world' since, as in the case of Adam, a single human being can be the progenitor of a whole world of other human beings. And it is the 'world' that the individual is obliged to say was created for his sake.

The same kind of ambivalence is to be observed in another Talmudic passage[17] relevant to our theme. The passage reads:

Our Rabbis taught: if one sees a crowd of Israelites,[18] he recites the benediction: Blessed is He who is wise in secrets, for just as no two faces are exactly alike so, too, no two minds are exactly alike. Ben Zoma once saw a crowd on a step on the Temple mount, whereupon he recited: Blessed is He who is wise in secrets and blessed is He who created all these to serve me. He used to say: What labours Adam had to perform before he could eat his bread. He had to plough, to sow, to reap, to bind the sheaves, to thresh, to winnow, to select the ears, to grind them, to sift the flour, to knead the dough and bake it, and only then could he eat; whereas when I arise I find all these have been done for me. And how many labours Adam had to carry out before he could put on clothes. He had to shear, to wash the wool, to comb it, to spin it and weave it, and only then could he have a garment to wear; whereas when I arise I find all these things have been done for me. All kinds of people come early to the door of my house, and I rise in the morning to find all these before me.

In this passage, while the uniqueness of every individual is stressed – no two faces in the crowd are exactly alike and no two minds, God alone knowing the 'secrets' of each – the interdependence of human beings is also stressed. Ben Zoma blesses God for creating the diversity to be observed among human beings and also blesses God for creating so many to serve him. But, it is obviously implied, each of those who serve Ben Zoma is himself served in this way by others.

In other Talmudic passages, too, the significance of the world is invoked in the very process of stressing the importance and uniqueness of the individual. R Meir said[19] that the whole world was created for the sake of the scholar who studies the Torah for its own sake. Of the miracle-working saint, R Haninah b. Dosa, it is said that a Heavenly voice used to proclaim: 'The whole world is sustained in the merit of Haninah My son.'[20] On the verse, 'Let us hear the conclusion of the whole matter, fear God, and keep His commandments, for this is the whole of man' (Ecclesiastes 12:13), two comments are made by Rabbis;[21] one understanding the verse to mean that the whole world was created for the sake of the saintly man (who 'fears God, and keeps His commandments'), the other, that the whole world was created to be a companion to this kind of man.

This interdependence between the individual and the 'world' prevents an understanding of the passages mentioned as expressing a Jewish version of Nietzsche's Superman. In *Aḥad ha-'Am*'s famous attack on Micah Joseph Berdichewsky (1865–1921), who argued for a transvaluation of values in which all are made subordinate to the Superman, the ideal type for which the whole human race exists,[22] *Aḥad ha-'Am* admits that Judaism knows of the idea of a Superman but such a type is, in Judaism, one who serves humanity not one who is served by humanity. *Aḥad ha-'Am* quotes the above passages in support of his view but he fails to appreciate that, in the Talmud, no such clear and precise distinctions are made. It is certainly going too far to say, as '*Aḥad ha-'Am* does, that, according to these Talmudic passages, the saint was not created for others but, on the contrary, is an end in himself. Each individual is, in one sense, an end in himself but, in Rabbinic thinking, this does not warrant the conclusion that he was not created for others.

Aḥad ha-'Am refers, also, to the Hasidic Zaddik as the spiritual Superman who is the apex of creation in Hasidic thought. But, as Martin Buber rightly points out,[23] the Hasidic ideal is to begin with the self but not end there. Buber quotes the tale of the Zaddik of Zanz who said to another Zaddik that the fact that he had grown old and had still not atoned for his sins ate at his heart, whereupon his colleague replied, 'O my friend you are thinking only of yourself.

How about forgetting yourself and thinking of the world?' Buber sees in this something more than a reassurance by the friend of the Zanzer that he greatly overrates his sins. As Buber paraphrases it, the friend is saying in quite a general sense: 'Do not keep worrying about what you have done wrong, but apply the soul-power you are now wasting on self-reproach to such active relationship to the world as you are destined for. You should not be occupied with yourself but with the world.'

Buber, as a Jewish religious existentialist, is grappling with the problem of the other that is so bound to be of concern to existentialist philosophers with their preoccupation with the authenticity of the self. Kierkegaard, in particular, discerns different attitudes to the individual self in Judaism and Christianity. Kierkegaard comments on 'Two women will be grinding at the mill; one is taken and the one is left' (Matthew 24:41):[24]

> What a fearful separation and isolation! What a difference from paganism and Judaism, where the family and then the town and then the province and then the country participate in the individual, so that, for example, when a man distinguishes himself then immediately the family, the town, the province and the country share in his fame. Whereas Christianity means the separation of the individual, paganism and Judaism means the supreme power of the category of the race and the generation.

Kierkegaard, in his typically broad generalization, is fair neither to Judaism and paganism on the one hand nor to Christianity on the other, as if such problems can be reduced to neat categorization. Even the most extreme versions of existentialism cannot escape the problem of the 'other'. As Jaspers puts it,[25] 'The human being cannot become human by himself. Self-being is only real in connection with another self-being. Alone, I sink into gloomy isolation – only in communication with others can I be revealed.'[26]

More than any other contemporary Jewish thinker, Abraham Chen,[27] without mentioning Kierkegaard, turns the tables on the Danish thinker in seeing Judaism rather than Christianity as strongly individualistic, but Chen is as one-sided as Kierkegaard. S. J. Sevin, in his Introduction to Chen's book *be-Malkhut ha-Yahadut*, remarks that he had heard Chen tell more than once this tale regarding the Hasidic Zaddik Levi Yitzhak of Berditchev. (Sevin is doubtful whether anyone can accept the implications of the tale but he admires Chen both for telling it and for the one-sidedness that can perhaps help to redress the balance.) R Levi Yitzhak, one Yom

Kippur, was acting as the prayer-leader. Towards the end of the long day of prayer and fasting, his disciples observed that the Zaddik was prolonging his prayers with such sweet melodies and with such yearning that they had a profound sense that something unutterably awesome was about to take place. But suddenly the Zaddik stopped for a moment and then rushed through the service and quickly sent the people home to break the fast. Afterwards, R Levi Yitzhak explained that he sensed that the time was opportune for God to be entreated to send the Messiah to redeem the world and he knew that if he persisted in his fervent prayers he could, indeed, bring about the advent of the Messiah. But then he noticed an old man who would not dream of leaving the synagogue to break his fast until the service was at an end and he sensed that if that were to happen the old man would certainly die. So the Zaddik's dilemma was whether to continue to pray and to succeed in bringing the Messiah or whether to rush through the prayers so that the old man might live. He came to the conclusion that his immediate duty was to save the life of the old man even if this meant postponing the advent of the Messiah for a long long time.

CHAPTER 2

Self-realization as a religious value

The statement in the Mishnah, quoted in the previous chapter, that it is necessary for a man to say, 'For my sake was the world created', is not, of course, an invitation to megalomania. Unbridled self-esteem and self-centredness is as stultifying as complete disregard for one's own interests. The famous maxim attributed to Hillel (*Avot* 1:14) is pertinent: 'If I am not for myself who is for me? But if I am only for myself what am I?', as is the saying of the blind Hasidic master R Simhan Bunem of Psycha. This teacher observed that a man should have two pockets, in each of which he places a slip of paper. On one slip he should inscribe the words of the Mishnah, 'For my sake was the world created', on the other the plea of Abraham, 'I am but dust and ashes' (Genesis 18:27). When a man begins to doubt his worth, when he sees himself surrendering to despair, he should take out the slip reminding him that the whole world was created for his sake. But when he is at risk of thinking too much of himself he should read the inscription on the other slip as a reminder that even an Abraham thought of himself as but dust and ashes in the eyes of the Almighty.

In the same vein this Hasidic master used to say that he often entertained the notion, how good it would be if he could change places with Abraham. He would be Abraham, no less, and Abraham would be 'the blind Bunem'. But then, he reflected, how would such an exchange benefit the Almighty? Before the exchange, God would have in His world an Abraham and a blind Bunem and after the exchange had been effected God would still have an Abraham and a blind Bunem. In other words, God requires, as it were, each individual in his uniqueness.[1]

In this chapter the idea is explored to what extent Judaism acknowledges that a man has a duty to himself.

It has to be said right away that the whole notion of a man having a duty to himself is notoriously difficult. The very idea of duty implies an obligation *on* the self. How, then, can the self have a duty to the self? Yet it can be argued that in a theistic philosophy a man does have a duty to himself, an obligation *to God* to realize his full potential. The question to be considered, then, is whether, in the Jewish tradition, there is to be found the idea of a religious duty of self-realization.

From the early Rabbinic period, duties (*mitzvot*) have been classified as those between man and God (*ben adam le-makom*) and those between man and his neighbour (*ben adam le-ḥavero*).[2] It should be noted that the obligation with regard to both groupings is a religious one. Those in both groups are *mitzvot*, divine commands, religious duties. The difference is solely in connection with the object to which they are directed, not in the nature of the obligation. It is, consequently, somewhat lacking in precision to translate or paraphrase the obligations between man and his neighbour as 'ethical obligations', though this is often done. A more precise definition would be, religious duties with an ethical direction or aim.

Nowhere in the early literature is there found a third grouping, that of *mitzvot ben adam le-'atzmo*, 'duties a man owes to himself', i.e. that there exists a religious obligation for a man to engage in the task of self-realization.[3] The concept of a third category, duties a man owes to himself, is, like the term itself, of mediaeval vintage and is not found anywhere in the Jewish sources until the late mediaeval period. It is worthwhile to inquire when and why this new concept was introduced into Jewish thought.

So far as I have been able to discover, the first Jewish thinker to speak of a third category of *mitzvot*, those between a man and himself (*mitzvot ben adam le-'atzmo*), is Joseph Albo (d. 1444) in his *Sefer ha-'Ikkarim*.[4] Significantly enough, Albo puts the new threefold, instead of twofold, division of *mitzvot* into the mouth of a Christian scholar. Albo begins this chapter in his book (heavily censored in later editions of the work) by referring to a discussion he had engaged in with this Christian scholar, who argued for the superiority of Christianity over Judaism.

According to the Christian scholar, as Albo reports him, a religion (*torah*) should embrace three categories, i.e. it should possess three types of rules (*mitzvot*): (1) those between man and God, (2) those between man and his neighbour (for those two Albo employs the standard Rabbinic terminology) and (3) those between man and himself. Albo, quoting the Christian scholar, refers to these three, based on the Latin, respectively, as: (1) *ceremoniales* (2) *judiciales* (3) *morales*.[5] The Christian finds Judaism defective in all three categories; in the third because Judaism, unlike Christianity, only commands right actions and is indifferent, so he argues, to purity of heart. Albo springs to the defence of Judaism, declaring that, in fact, Judaism is the superior faith in all three categories. With regard to the third category, the obligations a man has to himself, Albo remarks:

The charge of imperfection he advances against the moral principles, the third part of the Torah, on the grounds that the Torah of Moses only commands right action but not purity of heart, the truth is the exact opposite. For the Torah says: 'Circumcise therefore the foreskin of your heart' (Deuteronomy 10:16); 'And thou shalt love the Lord thy God with all thy heart' (Deuteronomy 6:5); 'And thou shalt love thy neighbour as thyself' (Leviticus 19:18); 'But thou shalt fear thy God' (Leviticus 19:14); 'Thou shalt not take vengeance, nor bear any grudge against the children of thy people' (Leviticus 19:18). The reason it commands right action is because purity of heart is of no account unless practice is in agreement with it. The important thing, however, is intention. David says: 'Create in me a clean heart, O God' (Psalm 51:12). And there are many other passages of the same kind, more than we can enumerate here.

Albo's list here actually covers only the two conventional categories but his reasoning appears to be that the third category follows on the other two. By observing the ceremonial laws and by keeping the laws between man and man, the third type of *mitzvot*, those having to do with self-realization and self-perfection, is achieved. In fact, it looks as if Albo's third category corresponds to Bahya Ibn Pakudah's *Duties of the Heart*; Bahya's book, influenced by Sufism in this and other matters, being the source for this passage and Albo's treatment of the theme.[6]

A century and a half after Albo, R Samuel Edels (1555–1631), the *Maharsha*, in his celebrated Commentary to the Aggadot of the Talmud, seeks artificially to read into a Talmudic passage the idea of a man having a duty to himself.[7] In the passage the Talmud records three opinions on the matters to be stressed by one who wishes to become exceedingly pious or saintly (*ḥasida*). These three are: *nezikin* ('damages', i.e. tractate *Nezikin*, dealing with relations between man and his fellows, including the obligation to prevent harm being caused to others); *avot* ('fathers', i.e. tractate *Avot*, 'Ethics of the Fathers'); and *berakhot* ('blessings', i.e. tractate

Berakhot, dealing with prayer and benedictions). According to the *Maharsha*, these three correspond to the three categories of perfection towards which the candidate for saintliness ought to aspire. *Nezikin* and *berakhot* refer to the conventional Rabbinic division – 'between man and man' and 'between man and God' – whereas *avot* refers to the third category. But the *Maharsha*, obviously thinking of another Talmudic passage,[8] in which the terms used are 'good to Heaven' and 'good to [other] creatures', formulates it as: 'A man's good deeds are of three kinds, good to Heaven, good to [other] creatures and good to himself [*tov le-'atzmo*]'. Thus, in the *Maharsha*'s interpretation, the kind of ethical conduct described in tractate *Avot* has as its aim self-perfection in the sense of sound character development.

A contemporary of the *Maharsha*, R Isaiah Horowitz (d. 1630), in his *Sheney Luḥot ha-Berit* (abbreviated *Shelah*), similarly speaks of a man's obligations to himself, discussing this in his encyclopaedic work under the general heading of *derekh eretz*[9] ('the way of the earth'), the Rabbinic term for, among other things, good conduct and correct behaviour. This is how the *Shelah* defines it:

> The meaning of *derekh eretz* is correct behaviour, extraordinary humility, improvement of the character and all delightful things, to love all creatures and be loved by them, to be a man of peace and a perfect man, contributing to the world in general and in particular in both spiritual and worldly matters. *Derekh eretz* is conducted in three ways: (1) the way of perfect conduct by a man for himself; (2) the way of perfect conduct for a man in his home; (3) the way of perfect conduct by a man in relation to his fellows.

Each of these, continues the *Shelah*, should be pursued in three ways: in connection with wealth, with body and with soul. He then proceeds to demonstrate how man should strive for self-perfection in these three areas.

Self-perfection of the soul means, in the *Shelah's* analysis, that a man should ever be aware of his soul's elevated nature, seeking at all times to strengthen his soul to contemplate the wonders of God's creation and to worship Him in truth. He should appreciate that it is through the soul that knowledge of God is attained and he must therefore make his body subservient to his soul. But physical self-perfection must also be cultivated; the Rabbis' teaching is that it is forbidden for us to endanger our health. The body must be cared for adequately; it should be bathed regularly, generally kept clean and everything repulsive kept away from it. The hair and beard should be kempt and neat. The way a man dresses and the manner in which he works are also relevant to physical self-perfection. Self-perfection also includes an acceptance of a man's intellectual abilities or lack of them so that he should not try to grasp matters beyond his ken and he should make progress in his studies step by step. As for self-perfection with regard to wealth, this obviously implies that a man should not be a spendthrift. He should take care to earn an honest living and when God gives him worldly goods and possessions he should look after them by investing his money in profitable business ventures. He should strive to be self-supporting and not rely on financial assistance given to him by others as an act of charity.[10]

The paucity of reference to the third category is evident. In Albo the whole category is really taken over from the Christian scholar on the principle of anything you can do we can do better. Even in the *Maharsha* and the *Shelah* the treatment hardly proceeds very far from teachings in the traditional sources. Concepts such as self-esteem, self-respect and self-fulfilment, though no doubt owing much to ancient Greek ideas about the nature of the good life, are basically modern, the fruit of the Renaissance and the resulting increasingly man-centred universe. The ancient Jewish sources were too theologically motivated to admit into their scheme the idea of self-expression as an end in itself or even as a religious obligation. It is noteworthy that in the writings of all three thinkers we have examined the Godward direction is always prominent. For Albo the third category is one of *mitzvah*, divine command. For the *Maharsha* it belongs to the way of saintliness. For the *Shelah* it is part of the kind of self-perfection that leads to God. To be sure, for all three authors the aim is that of self-fulfilment but the self to be fulfilled is the self created in God's image and the fulfilment itself solely in obedience to a divine command. That is why some Jewish mystics can speak paradoxically of self-transcendence as the highest form of self-fulfilment.[11]

For all that, the recognition that the traditional sources do not acknowledge the humanistic or secular view of self-realization certainly does not mean that they ignore individual strivings for perfection. They patently do not. From all that has been said in this chapter, it is clear that the individual *qua* individual counts, according to Judaism, in the eyes of God.

CHAPTER 3

Attitudes to life and death

Although each individual is given in Judaism a large degree of autonomy he is never seen as so completely in control of his own life that he is allowed to dispose of it at will. Suicide is a very serious offence in Jewish law.[1]

It is to be noted that there is no direct prohibition of suicide in the Torah as there is for murder ('Thou shalt not kill' in the Decalogue: Exodus 20:13 and Deuteronomy 5:17). In the Talmud,[2] however, the prohibition is arrived at by a process of exegesis on the verse, 'And surely your blood of your lives will I require' (Genesis 9:5), interpreted as, 'I will require your blood if you yourselves shed it.' It is possible that there is no direct prohibition because very few people of sound mind would be inclined to commit suicide in any event.

It follows from this that suicide and murder are two separate offences in the Jewish tradition. Suicide is not homicide and is not covered by 'Thou shalt not kill' in the Decalogue. In the Rabbinic classification of duties, referred to in the previous chapter, homicide would be considered an offence both 'between man and God' and 'between man and man' whereas suicide would fall only under the former heading. Maimonides[3] states that, while murder is a capital offence, suicide is not and incurs only the penalty of 'death by the hands of Heaven'.[4]

It is not only actual suicide that is strictly forbidden. Any lack of care for one's health or any risk to life through activities which can be dangerous are forbidden under the heading of suicide. In the Talmudic maxim[5] 'danger to life is to be treated more severely than that which is [otherwise] forbidden', i.e. even where the law permits a risk to be taken with regard to religious law (e.g. in the case of forbidden food) it does not allow the same risk to be taken where life is at stake. If, say, there are ten parcels of meat, nine kosher and one forbidden, and one of them is found separated from the others, so that it is not known whether this is one of the nine kosher parcels or is the one forbidden, it is permitted to eat that meat because the law relies on probability. But if there are ten cups of wine, only one of which contains poison, it is still forbidden to drink from any of the cups. The reasoning behind this rule is fairly clear. In the matter of religious law, since the law allows reliance on the probability principle, the meat eaten is kosher even if, so to speak, it is, in reality, forbidden meat. Kosher and non-kosher depends on the legal procedures to be adopted. But, in the case of the cups of wine, the probability principle cannot be relied upon since, legal procedure or no legal procedure, if the cup imbibed contains poison it will kill. Maimonides,[6] following the Talmud, states:

> There are many things which the Sages declared forbidden because they may endanger life. Anyone who offends in this way, saying, 'it is my own life that I am endangering, what business is it of anyone else?' or, 'I do not care', is to be given the flogging of rebellion [*makkat mardut*, the term used for a flogging imposed by Rabbinic law].

Maimonides proceeds to list these Rabbinic prohibitions such as drinking wine left uncovered overnight into which a snake may have injected its venom.

May an individual pray to God that he should die? While the Halakhic sources do discuss whether it is permitted for others to pray that an incurable in great pain should be released from his sufferings by death, there is hardly any discussion on whether a man tired of his life, though forbidden to commit suicide, may ask God to take his life.

The two questions are quite distinct. Even if it be argued that it is not permitted to pray that another human being should die, it can still be argued that it is permitted for a man to pray that he himself should die, since in the first instance the prayer is directed against another, albeit for his supposed advantage, whereas in the second it is directed only against the self. Conversely, even if it be argued that it is permitted to pray for the speedy death of another who is in severe pain, it does not follow that it is permitted for a man to pray for his own death, since in the one instance compassion comes into play whereas in the other it might be held that it is better for the sufferer to bear his pain with as much equanimity as he can summon in order for God's will for him to be done. Again, even if it be argued that it is permitted for a sufferer to pray for his own death, would this apply even if there is hope for a later improvement in the sufferer's condition and would it apply to severe mental as well as physical suffering? In other words, should an individual ever pray to God, 'I cannot stand it any longer. I have had enough. Please take my life and release me from my anguish.'

On the question of prayers that an incurable suffering great pain should die, R Nissim Gerondi, the *Ran* (d.*c.* 1375), understands a Talmudic passage[7] to mean not only that this is permitted but that it is meritorious. The *Ran* finds support for his view from the story of the maid-servant of Rabbi Judah the Prince.[8] When Rabbi Judah was on his deathbed and in great distress because of his sufferings, the maid-servant entreated God to take his life, and her attitude was evidently approved of by the Rabbis. Many centuries later, the problem was discussed by the Turkish Rabbi, Hayyim Palaggi (1788–1869), who follows the *Ran* in permitting such prayers.[9] A contemporary Halakhist, R Eliezer Waldinberg (b. 1917), argues from the silence of the Codes on the matter that they would not permit it and even those authorities who might permit it would only do so if the prayers were offered by strangers. If members of the family were permitted to pray for the death of one of the family, their motivation might be selfish in order to be released from having to care for him.[10]

The only reference to our question, whether the individual may pray for his own death, that I have been able to discover is not in a Halakhic work at all but in the Commentary to the Torah, *Mey ha-Shiloaḥ*,[11] by the Hasidic master, R Mordecai Joseph of Izbica (d. 1854).[12] R Mordecai Joseph's comment is on the verse, 'Thou shalt not sacrifice unto the Lord thy God an ox, or a sheep, wherein is a blemish, even any evil thing; for that is an abomination unto the Lord thy God' (Deuteronomy 17:1). Prayer, he observes, is in place of the sacrifices in Temple times. The reference in the verse is, then, to blemished, stupid prayers. There are two types of blemished prayer, an abomination to God. These are the 'ox' type of prayer and the 'sheep' type of prayer. The 'ox' type is when a man, attacked by his opponents in religious matters, prays to God to punish them. In the Kabbalah the ox is the symbol of *Gevurah*, 'stern judgement'. It is utterly wrong for a man to invoke the power of the divine judgements against his foes even if there is the strongest conviction that he is in the right. The blemished 'sheep' type of prayer goes to the opposite extreme. This type is when a man, struggling for the truth against seemingly overwhelming odds, gives in mentally and entreats God to release him from the struggle by allowing him to die. This is a cowardly surrender to utter despair, 'like the prayer of Jonah and Elijah' this author adds.

Jonah's prayer, to which the author alludes, is, of course, that contained in the verse, 'Therefore now, O Lord, take, I beseech thee, my life from me; for it is better for me to die than to live' (Jonah 4:4). The similar prayer by Elijah is in the verse, 'But he himself went a day's journey into the wilderness, and came and sat down under a broom-tree; and he requested for himself that he might die; and said, "It is enough; now, O Lord, take away my life; for I am not better than my fathers"' (1 Kings 19:4). Both the prophets uttered their plea for death when their mission seemed to have failed. R Mordecai reads the two narratives as expressing disapproval of their attitudes.

In the second volume of his Commentary[13] R Mordecai Joseph elaborates on the theme. Here he remarks that the good man should not take his distress at the deeds of sinners so much to heart as to wish that he were to be no longer alive to witness their sinful deeds. We know that R Mordecai Joseph, a former disciple of the Kotzker Rebbe, breaking with his master to found his own Hasidic dynasty,[14] suffered greatly from the taunts of the followers of the Kotzker, who persecuted him for his effrontery, as they saw it, in defying the master to formulate his own Hasidic philosophy. He was also a very unconventional Hasidic master, defending, for example, in his *Mey ha-Shiloaḥ*, even some of the villains of Scripture as no mere profligates but as great men with great faults and, on the other hand, as we have seen, he was not averse to criticizing some of the Biblical heroes. Not surprisingly, therefore, his comments are evidently addressed, in part at least, to himself. He is urging the man attacked for his unusual theories to yield neither to despair nor to asking God to take his side.

R Mordecai Joseph does not refer to Moses' prayer, 'I am not able to bear all this people myself alone, because it is too heavy for me. And if Thou deal thus with me, kill me, I pray Thee, out of hand, if I have found favour in thy sight; and let me not look upon my wretchedness' (Numbers 11:14–15), possibly because Moses asks God to kill him only 'if' he is asked to shoulder a burden too heavy for him to bear. Moses does not despair of his worth to declare that his life is valueless. He does no more than protest that he cannot accept a task beyond his capacity. In this R Mordecai Joseph differs from David Kimhi, the *Redak* (1160–1235) who, in his Commentary to Jonah, does compare the prayer of Jonah with that of Moses and holds that both were not cries of despair but came from the heart of prophets who loved their people and could not bear to witness the sufferings they believed would come upon that people. Abraham Ibn Ezra (1989–1164), in his Commentary to Jonah, understands Jonah's prayer in much the same way. Even in Kimhi and Ibn Ezra, for all the emphasis on the people, as in the Biblical verses, Jonah appears as an individual facing his own fate. Centuries later, in R Mordecai Joseph, the individual motif is so stressed that the prophets Jonah and Elijah can serve as prototypes of individual strivings in the quest for God.

CHAPTER 4

Family relationships

The family both circumscribes and broadens the horizons of its members, each individual member having a dual role, as a person in his or her own right and as father or mother, son or daughter, brother or sister, husband or wife, with the extended relationships of grandparents, grandchildren, uncles, aunts, nephews, nieces, cousins, parents-in-law, children-in-law, step-parents and step-children.

In the Jewish tradition, these family relationships are carefully graded so that the closer the relationship the greater the degree of personal responsibility. Thus in Jewish law the mourning rites to be observed on the death of a near relative are limited to the seven closest relatives: father, mother, son, daughter, brother, sister, husband, wife. Of these seven, the mourning period for a parent extends for a whole year while for the other five for one month.[1] Maimonides[2] remarks that to fail to observe the mourning rites for a near relative is to be 'cruel', i.e. it is evidence that the loving relationship that ought to have been present when the relative was alive was totally absent. The individual who fails to mourn the loss of a near relative has a deficiency in his character. By allowing his individuality to gain so completely the upper hand as to sever his family relationship he diminishes that very individuality.

Similarly, with regard to almsgiving, the nearer a relative the greater an obligation to assist him when he is in need. Poor parents take precedence over other relatives, closer members of the family over more distant relatives and members of the family over strangers.[3]

The duty to respect other members of the family is similarly graded. The fifth commandment, 'Honour thy father and thy mother', obligates children to honour their parents. Respect for the father takes precedence over respect for the mother unless the parents are divorced, in which case the son can please himself to which of the two he gives precedence.[4] A step-father and step-mother are to be respected as an extension of the obligation to honour parents.[5] Other extensions are by younger siblings to older,[6] to father-in-law and mother-in-law[7] and to grandparents, although the respect due to parents takes precedence over that due to grandparents.[8]

Isserles in the *Shulḥan 'Arukh*[9] records the famous Responsum of R Joseph Colon, the *Maharik* (d. 1480),[10] where this authority rules that the fifth commandment does not obligate a son to give up the woman he wishes to marry because of parental opposition to the match. In support of his far-reaching ruling, the *Maharik* advances three reasons. There is a debate in the Talmud[11] on the rule that a son is obliged to give his parents food, drink and clothes. Does this mean that a son is obliged to provide his parents with these out of his pocket or does it mean only that the son should, where necessary, act as a waiter or a valet to his parents? This is debated in the Talmud where the conclusion is that a son is not obliged to support his parents financially (unless they are poor and the son rich[12]). Since the son is not obliged to give up his wealth for his parents, argues the *Maharik, a fortiori* he has no obligation to give up the woman of his choice at his parents' whim. Secondly, since it is forbidden for a man to marry a woman without first seeing her, because he may come to dislike her, this shows that it is the will of God for husband and wife to love one another, so that, it can be argued, for a father to order his son to give up a woman the son loves amounts to an order by a parent to his child to transgress a prohibition of the Torah and such orders must not be obeyed. Thirdly, argues the *Maharik*, even according to those who hold that a son is obliged to provide his parents with food, drink and clothing out of his pocket, this applies only to where, as in the case of food, drink and clothing, the parent asks for his own needs to be satisfied. The fifth commandment does not mean that a parent is entitled to issue any order he wishes and the son obliged to obey these orders. 'Honour thy father' does not mean 'Obey thy father'. Where a father asks his son, say, to pour him out a glass of tea, to take a trivial example, the son should do so because the request demonstrates the father's need not because the father orders it. It follows that where the father orders his son to give up the woman he wishes to marry, a matter of no direct concern to the father, it can be said to be none of the father's business.

Another illuminating illustration of how the Jewish tradition frees the individual from undue parental control is where a son disagrees with his father in matters of Jewish learning. Although the Talmud[13] states that a son must not disagree with his father's opinion, this has never been understood to mean that a Jewish scholar may not engage his father in debate in matters of Torah learning. R Hayyim Eleazar Spira of Munkacs (1872–1937), in a learned Responsum on the subject,[14] provides a detailed list of scholars throughout the ages who took issue with their fathers and teachers where they held them to be in the wrong.

The ruling of the *Maharik* has been considered at length because it has implications far beyond the strictly legal aspects of filial piety. What is involved is the question of where family loyalties end, of when these loyalties fill and enrich the life of the individual member and when they empty and impoverish it. In this area, for all the guidance provided by the law, it is ultimately a matter of individual choice.

A particularly vivid illustration of the problem is provided in the struggle of the burgeoning Hasidic movement in the eighteenth century with the *Mitnaggedim*, the traditional Rabbis and communal leaders, who opposed the movement as detrimental to faith and to communal responsibility.

Avigdor b. Hayyim, a fiery opponent of Hasidism, drew up a list of nineteen counts against the, to him, heretical sect for the consideration of the Russian authorities. Avigdor and his supporters believed that if his counts were substantiated they would prove conclusively the subversive nature of the sect as a threat to religion and to ordered society. Avigdor's twelfth count reads:

> They [the Hasidim] have no respect whatever for their parents. For, they argue, a father only brings his child into the world in order to satisfy his lusts and there is, consequently, no obligation for a child to honour its father. The same applies to the mother but [they say] some measure of respect is due to the mother from the heart of the child she suckled.[15]

Allowing for the bias of a deeply prejudiced observer, it would be a mistake to reject out of hand the contention that the Hasidim treated parental authority lightly. Indeed, this was one of the charges the Hasidim hardly bothered to refute. Thus R Shneor Zalman of Liady (1747–1813), founder of the *Ḥabad* tendency in Hasidism, in a letter to a non-Hasidic Rabbi,[16] defends the right of his youthful followers to disobey their parents, who objected to the young men offering their prayers in the newly established Hasidic conventicles where numerous changes had been introduced into the liturgy. R Shneor Zalman quotes the *Maharik* on the lack of any obligation to obey parents and applies it to justify the departure from tradition and from parental authority by the young men. As a movement of rebellion Hasidism could not allow itself to become stultified through the strictest interpretation of the fifth commandment. In this connection the story told of the Hasidic master, Israel of Ruzhyn (d. *c.* 1851), is very revealing. It is said that many heads of families in Berditchev tried to convince R Israel that it was his clear duty to persuade the young men, who had left their wives and families in order to become his disciples, to return home. The Rabbi told them of a man in the days of the Maggid of Meserich who had been compelled to give his young wife a divorce at the instigation of the Rabbi of the town and the wife's father because the young man spent too much time at the Maggid's centre. When the Messiah comes, declared R Israel, the young man, his father-in-law and the Rabbi of the town will be called to judgement. The Messiah will pronounce his decision. To the father-in-law he will say, 'You followed the Rabbi of the town and so you are justified.' To the Rabbi he will say, 'You took the law as your authority so you are justified.' He will add, however, 'But I have come for those who are not justified.'[17] In other words, even if the law can be interpreted, and rightly interpreted, to forbid the Hasidic attitude, a movement of rebellion cannot allow a law to be invoked where that law has the aim of reading the movement out of existence.

Parallels to this kind of conflict are not difficult to adduce among the movements of reform and rebellion in other religious traditions: in the 'Great retirement' of the Buddha abandoning his wife Gopa as she slept and renouncing the pleasures of his father's palace; of Jesus: 'For I am come to set a man at variance against his father, and the daughter against her mother, and the daughter-in-law against her mother-in-law' (Matthew 10:35), and his: 'Who is my mother? and who are my brethren?' (Matthew 12:48); of Mohammed as a posthumous child who lost his mother when he was six years of age. No man can succeed in the spiritual path, taught the Hasidic master, R Elimelech of Lizensk (1717–1787), until he rids himself of pride in his ancestry, hence Abraham, at the outset of his spiritual journey, was told to leave his father's house.[18] It is not surprising to find the Maggid of Meserich[19] teaching that the Torah enjoins us to honour parents, even though it might have been argued that all the indignities of man's situation are the result of the character defects he has inherited from his parents. The fifth commandment is to be seen as an injunction to see dignity even where there is no dignity, just as God's glory can be discerned, for those who have eyes to see, even in this world of error and confusion. Highly speculative though this is, is it not possible to see the development of the charismatic Hasidic master, the Zaddik, as in part, at least, due to the need of those who rebelled against their parents to find a substitute father-figure?

In the marriage relationship, too, as everyone knows, husband and wife have to surrender some of their individuality if the marriage is to work: 'Therefore shall a man leave his father and his mother, and shall cleave unto his wife, and they shall be one flesh' (Genesis 2:24). The second-century teacher, Ben Azai, for all his preaching the high value of the married state, could say that he could not marry because his soul desired the Torah as his love.[20] Although celibacy is normally frowned upon in Judaism, the *Shulḥan 'Arukh* can still rule[21] that where there is such strong love of the Torah the example of Ben Azai can be followed. On the verse, 'It is not good that the man should be alone: I will make him a help meet for him' (Genesis 2:18), the nineteenth-century Commentator, R Naftali Zvi Yehudah Berlin, observes[22] that the Hebrew for 'meet for him' is *kenegdo*, which can bear the meaning of 'opposed to him', yielding the thought that husband and wife are of 'help' to one another because of their differences, not in spite of them. And this applies to all family relationships. It is the variety of attitudes among the members of even the closest-knit family, the very conflict among persons of strong individuality, that cements the family bonds and enriches family life.

CHAPTER 5

Loving the neighbour

There can be very few Biblical texts so influential and yet so misunderstood as 'love thy neighbour as thyself' (Leviticus 19:18). In this chapter the various interpretations of the text in the Jewish tradition will be examined in so far as they are relevant to the particular theme of this book, the role of the individual in Judaism.

First to be noted is the plain meaning of the verse, that is, the original meaning in its context. It is astonishing that, throughout the ages, the second clause, 'love thy neighbour as thyself', has been detached from the rest of the verse to yield a completely different significance. The full verse reads: 'Thou shalt not take vengeance, nor bear any grudge against the children of thy people, but thou shalt love thy neighbour as thyself.' The Hebrew is *ve-ahavta*, correctly rendered as 'but thou shalt love'; the verse stating that, instead of taking vengeance against the neighbour and bearing him a grudge, one should act lovingly to him. In spite of the fact that he has behaved badly towards you, you should not be tempted to retaliate but should behave decently towards him. Furthermore, the Hebrew *le-re'akha* really means '*to* thy neighbour' not simply 'thy neighbour. And *kamokha* means '*who is* as thyself', i.e. 'as thyself' qualifies not the 'love' but the 'neighbour', the meaning being: behave lovingly towards him because he is like yourself, that is, with the same rights and feelings that you have. Thus, in the original context, the verse means, 'Even when someone has behaved badly towards you, try to overcome your desires for revenge but rather behave lovingly towards him because, after all, he too is a human being and a member of the covenant people and therefore entitled to be treated as you yourself wish to be treated.[1]

As in many other areas, however, the plain, original meaning of the text is not necessarily the meaning it bears in the long tradition of Jewish life and thought. In that tradition the second clause is taken on its own as a command to love the neighbour as the self, though, even here, it is the outcome of the love in deeds that is stressed rather than the loving feelings and emotions. It is difficult to see how emotions can be coerced by a command and whether, in any event, it makes sense to love someone else as oneself in the emotional sense. It is doubtful whether the expression 'as thyself' has much meaning in the emotional sense since the concept of 'love' involves in this sense a reaching out to another. To care for the self is one thing; for the self to *love* the self borders on the schizophrenic. And the verse was applied to all, even to those one has never known or seen and even to persons one dislikes. There is no need to make the dubious distinction between 'liking' and 'loving'. It is a moot point whether one can entertain loving feelings for a person one dislikes. But if love refers to loving *deeds* it is surely possible for a person to rise to the heights of behaving in a considerate fashion even to unlovable people. It may be impossible to love the unpleasant Dr Fell but he can be treated as a human being entitled to respect because he is created in God's image.

Maimonides, following earlier Jewish teachings, is careful to formulate it all as follows:[2]

> It is a religious duty [*mitzvah*] incumbent upon every man to love every one of Israel as his own self [*ke-gufo*], as it is said: 'thou shalt love thy neighbour as thyself'. It is necessary, therefore, to relate his praises and to have care for his money just as a man has care for his own money and wishes to be respected himself. But whoever achieves respect through the degradation of his neighbour has no share in the World to Come.[3]

Maimonides clearly understands 'as thyself' as qualifying 'love'; a man must love his neighbour as much as himself. But the meaning of this love, according to Maimonides, is expressed not in emotions but in deeds that demonstrate solicitude for the neighbour, singing his praises and having regard for his wealth and physical well-being.

Maimonides considers the neighbour who is to be 'loved' to be a fellow Jew. The verse speaks, in fact, of 'the children of thy people'. It has to be said that, on the whole, in the Jewish tradition, while there are many injunctions against treating Gentiles in an unfair or unworthy manner and while there are demands that poor Gentiles be supported by the Jewish community,[4] the command 'to love thy neighbour' applies only to the neighbour who is a Jew. A number of Jewish thinkers have, however, understood the expression 'thy neighbour' as referring to Gentiles as well as to Jews.[5]

In Maimonides' formulation the stress is on the neighbour as an individual (Maimonides uses the expression *kol eḥad ve-eḥad* ('every single one'). But in the Kabbalah the idea emerges of Israel as a mystical corporate body, the love of each individual Jew becoming *ahavat yisrael*, 'the love of Israel' in the sense of all Jews, the love of the Jewish people.[6] In the old gibe, the anti-Semite may hate the Jews but like individual Jews – some of whom are his 'best friends'. The Jew, on the other hand, loves the Jewish people but often cannot stand the sight of individual Jews.

It is also worth noticing that Maimonides speaks only of 'as he cares for his own wealth and honour', not that he should be mindful of his neighbour's interests to the same degree as his own. When it comes to a conflict of interests, the normal Jewish view is to give preference to the individual's own needs. The Mishnah[7] states that if a man has lost something and his father (and *a fortiori* a stranger) has lost something, his own loss takes precedence, i.e. he is not obliged, in trying to recover his father's loss, thereby to fail to recover his own. Of course, if he wishes, a man may decide to forgo his own right in favour of his neighbour's and, while such a course cannot be the rule of everyone, a man cannot go through life always insisting on his own rights. The Talmud[8] to the Mishnah referred to quotes two sayings of the early-third-century teacher, R Judah, in the name of his teacher, Rav. One saying has it that a man's own needs take precedence over the needs of others. This is derived from the verse, 'save that there shall be no poor among you' (Deuteronomy 15:4), understood to mean, you yourself have the prior right to prevent poverty coming to you. But the second saying adds that anyone who always insists on his own rights in order to avoid poverty will find that his attitude is self-defeating and he will eventually become poor; naturally so since no one will wish to have too many business dealings with the man who always puts his own interests to the fore. And in any event, the saintly person will rarely insist on his rights. In 'Ethics of the Fathers'[9] the man who says 'What is thine is thine and what is mine is thine' is described as a *ḥasid*, a 'saint'.

The most severe conflict between the needs of one individual and another is where a choice has to be made with regard to life itself. The Talmud[10] takes it for granted – this is said to be a *sevara*, sheer common sense – that a man may not save his life by killing another (except in self-defence where he is the would-be victim of aggression[11]). The case referred to in the Talmud is where a man is ordered by a local tyrant to kill another man and if he fails to do so his own life will be forfeit. It is said that the case came before the fourth-century Babylonian teacher, Rava, who said to the man ordered to commit the murder, 'Allow yourself to be killed and do not commit murder. How do you know that your blood is redder? Perhaps the blood of that man [the intended victim] is redder.' The great French Commentator, to the passage, *Rashi*, explains it in this way. While a man may commit a sin or a crime in order to save his life, the crime of murder must be an exception to the rule since this crime involves the taking of life. It is more important to live than to die through refusing to commit a sin. But where the crime is that of murder a life will be lost either way so that the question of life versus sin does not arise. The only justification for the man ordered to kill to commit the murder would be because *his* life is of greater value than that of the intended victim. But how can this ever be determined? How could anyone possibly know that 'his blood is redder', i.e. that his life is of greater value in God's eyes than that of another? Since this can never be known it must be obvious that the sixth commandment, 'Thou shalt not kill', must mean, even where you kill in order to save your life.

Asher Ginsberg (1856–1927), who wrote under the pen-name *Aḥad ha-'Am*, develops an argument[12] on the question of a life for a life with which I have taken issue elsewhere.[13] This author is at pains to make a very dubious distinction between the Christian ethic, based, according to him, on love, and the Jewish ethic, which he claims is based on justice. *Aḥad ha-'Am* cites the hypothetical case mentioned elsewhere in the Talmud.[14] Two men are in the wilderness, one of them having in his possession only enough water to save one of them from dying of thirst. Is the man with the water obliged to share it with his companion or is he allowed to keep it all for himself? This is debated by Rabbi Akiba and Ben Petura. Ben Petura holds that he must share the water with the other even though that would mean that both will die. His present duty is to share the water so that the other, too, will live a little while longer. But Rabbi Akiba disagrees, holding that his own life comes first. This, according to *Aḥad ha-'Am*, is the case of Sidney Carton in Dickens' *Tale of Two Cities*, who goes to the guillotine in order to save his neighbour's life, quoting 'Greater love hath no man than this, that a man lay down his life for his friends.'[15]

Aḥad ha-'Am maintains that Ben Petura's view accords well with the Christian ethic in which love is paramount. But the Jewish view accords with that advanced by Rabbi Akiba. An ethic based on justice cannot tolerate a man giving up his life for another since justice is indivisible. Quoting Rava's ruling, as above, *Aḥad ha-'Am* declares that just as a man is not permitted to save his life by murdering another, because who knows of which the blood is redder, a man is not permitted to give his life for another (where, as in the case of the water, there is no question of murder) since, here, his blood may be the redder.

The truth of the matter is that *Aḥad ha-'Am* has totally confused the issue. In the case of the water it is obvious that there can be no *obligation* for the man who has the water to give it to his companion. If there were such an obligation the companion would be obliged to return the water, which is absurd. Even Ben Petura would agree. The question discussed by Ben Petura and Rabbi Akiba is whether the man who has the water is obliged to share it. Here Ben Petura holds that he does have an obligation to share the water even though both will die as a result, while Rabbi Akiba holds that it cannot be right for both to die where one can live. The very different question, whether the man with the water can choose to give it to the other because he believes the other's life is of greater value, is not discussed at all. It can be argued that a saintly individual commits an act of great merit as well as of great fortitude by giving up his life for another and in the process endowing his own life with a value greater than any it could have had if he had not sacrificed it. To say that Judaism positively objects to such saintly conduct is to reduce the Jewish ethic to pedestrianism. I would maintain that, just as it is axiomatic, to Rava, that a man must not kill another in order to save his life, it is axiomatic that where murder does not enter into it a man may, if he has good reason so to do, give up his life for others and that the Gospel saying, 'Greater love hath no man than this', does not belong to any specific Christian doctrine but demonstrates that such a course was held to be admirable by *Jews* in the time of Jesus.

But does not the man who gives up his life commit the crime of suicide? Not so. For suicide is a crime only because a life is taken whereas here the life of the other is saved through the act of suicide, unlike in Rava's case where, once life has been measured against life, the act is one of murder.[16]

In this area, too, it can be seen that Judaism allows considerable freedom to the individual in his relationship with his neighbour.

Aḥad ha-'Am is right when he observes in his essay, 'All men, including the self, are under obligation to develop their lives and their faculties to the limit of their capacity, and, at the same time, each is under obligation to assist his neighbour's self-development, as far as he can.' He is wrong when he continues, 'But just as I have no right to ruin another man's life for the sake of my own, so I have no right to ruin my own life for the sake of another's. Both of us are men, and both our lives have the same value *before the throne of justice*' (italics mine). The classical Jewish sources speak of value in the sight of God not 'before the throne of justice', a concept *Aḥad ha-'Am* has introduced, as a secular ethicist, in obedience to his supposed distinction between an ethic based on love and one based on justice. The history of Judaism knows of examples of men who gave their lives that others may live because they believed it is this that God, in whose eyes all are, indeed, equal, would have them do. It is surely perverse to categorize these 'fools of God' as sinners.

CHAPTER 6

Communal obligations

Each individual, apart from his relationships with other individuals and in his family, has group affiliations of one sort or another. The closest of these wider associations, so far as Judaism is concerned, is the Jewish community as a whole – *'Am Yisrael* – and this, in turn, is divided into particular communities, each of which is known as the *Kehilah* ('assembly') or, in Eastern Europe, the *Kahal*. Another name for the community in a particular place is the *tzibbur*. In modern times the *tzibbur* often consists of the smaller unit organized around a particular synagogue. To take the example of Anglo-Jewry, an individual may belong to a particular synagogue, to which he pays membership dues, and the synagogue may be affiliated to a particular movement, Orthodox or Reform or Liberal or Masorti. Each individual Jew is, in turn, part of the wider Anglo-Jewish community, represented by the Board of Deputies. As a Jew, he is also a member of the Jewish people with duties and responsibilities to Jews everywhere but especially in the State of Israel, which, of course, has its own national structures. Human nature being what it is, tensions are bound to arise between the individual, with his own interests, and the communities of which he is part, as they will arise between the smaller units and the greater.[1]

In the tightly knit Jewish communities in the middle ages, there was little possibility for the individual to free himself from communal control. In addition to the powerful social disapproval of dissent and approval of conformity, in extreme cases the community could impose the *ḥerem*, the dreaded ban, to make the non-conformist virtually an outcast until he submitted.[2] Nowadays, the ban is never invoked, except perhaps among tiny extremist circles. And social approval and disapproval are effective only in a community the individual does not join of his own free choice and which he cannot freely leave if he is dissatisfied. Moreover, generally speaking, Jewish communities are conducted on democratic lines,[3] each member having a vote, although, it has to be said, in the majority of Orthodox synagogues there is no women's suffrage so that the female individual member does suffer disadvantages. But this latter belongs to the more general question, much discussed and debated nowadays,[4] of sexual equality in Judaism.

As for membership of the Jewish people, the legal position is that this can never be forfeited, even if the individual Jew gives up all religion or embraces another religion. In the middle ages a Talmudic passage[5] was relied upon to convey this idea of once a Jew always a Jew. The Talmudic passage is a comment on the verse, 'Israel hath sinned' (Joshua 7:11). Since the verse does not say 'the people hath sinned' but 'Israel hath sinned' (Israel being a more elevated title than 'the people'), the conclusion is drawn: 'even when it has sinned Israel remains Israel'. In the middle ages, this originally purely homiletical saying, was extended to mean that an Israelite always remains an Israelite come what may.[6] It has been said,[7] that the Jewish community is a club which it is almost impossible to resign from. But this is not strictly correct. Whatever the purely legal view, the majority of Jews do consider membership of the Jewish people to have lapsed when an individual voluntarily surrenders his Jewish identity. And, of course, a non-Jew, who freely chooses to become a member of the community, once he has undergone the conversion procedures, is a full member of the community.[8]

If the club analogy is to be used and is not too banal, it can all be put in this way. Judaism is like the philosophy of a club with a particular purpose over and above the purely social. The founder members of the club all belong to the same family as do the majority of its present-day membership but membership is open to all who accept the club's particular philosophy. Full membership is granted to these after a solemn initiation ceremony and they then enjoy full rights and privileges. The club's constitution contains a large number of strict rules. Some of the members adhere lovingly to these and tend to look askance on the members who disregard the rules. Other members press for a revision of the rules and still others quietly neglect some of them. Once a person has become a member, he is held to be a member for life, even if he no longer pays his dues, attends meetings or obeys any of the rules. He is a member *in absentia* and will always be welcomed back. It is only when he joins a club which has a contrary philosophy that his fellow members consider his membership to have lapsed.

The individual's quest for identity in the face of vast impersonal forces is assisted by the stress on community in Jewish life. Even the most fervent 'loner' diminishes himself unless, on the happy and tragic occasions in his life, he can give expression to his deepest emotions in the group to which he belongs; meeting his God, if he is religious, through participation in the religious ceremonies of that group. The institution of the *minyan*, the quorum of ten required for some of the Jewish prayers and rituals, is intended for this very purpose. A Jew marries in a congregation, he rejoices in a congregation when he is blessed with children and when he is laid to rest his son recites the Kaddish in a congregation.[9] Even the Jewish mystics, craving for an intense personal relationship with their God, felt the need to organize themselves into brotherhoods[10] to assist them in their quest. Even 'loners' appear to have a need to be 'joiners' at times. In this area, as in the others we have considered, the individual can feel his need for solitude threatened by his association with others but sanity demands not that he seeks to live as if only he existed but that he looks upon the group to which he belongs as helping him in his individuality. Needless to say, an individual should seek to belong, as far as is possible, to a group of like-minded people, which is why for example, the Hasidim became split into different sects or groupings, each with its own philosophy. The Karliner Hasidim used to render the hymn, 'Happy are we, how good is our portion, how pleasant is our lot, how beautiful is our heritage', '*How good is our portion* since we are Jews and not Gentiles; *how pleasant is our lot* since we are Hasidim and not *Mitnaggedim*; *how beautiful is our heritage* since we are Karliner Hasidim and not Hasidim belonging to other groupings within the movement.'

In the Rabbinic literature in particular the strongest emphasis is placed on the *tzibbur*, the community. Typical of the Rabbinic view are the statements about the *tzibbur* in tractate *Avot* ('Ethics of the Fathers') of the Mishnah. In a saying attributed to Rabban Gamaliel, son of R Judah the Prince, the ideal relationship between the individual worker for the community and the community he serves is expressed:[11] 'Let all who labour with the community labour with them for the sake of Heaven [i.e. not in order to gain power over others]. For the merit of their fathers is their support, and their righteousness stands for ever. And as for you [who work for the community] I grant you reward [God says] as if you had done it [on your own without the support given through the merit of their ancestors].' Travers Herford[12] is not far off the mark when he paraphrases this as:

None is to live for himself alone, or benefit by others without benefitting them in return. Every one therefore who 'works with the congregation' is to do so with no selfish motive, but 'for the sake of heaven', as a service rendered to God. What he does, with or on behalf of the congregation, is their act not his individual act; but the unselfish service thus rendered meets with the divine approval as if it were his own act.

Hillel is quoted as saying,[13] 'Do not separate yourself from the community' and, while undoubtedly there is in all this emphasis on the community a stern warning against sectarianism, Travers Herford[14] is here too conjectural when he suggests that Hillel is thinking of the Essenes, warning against a flight into the wilderness. In all probability these injunctions were directed against Jews, otherwise pious and observant, who tended to curry favour with the Gentile authorities at the expense of the Jewish community. It cannot be accidental that Rabban Gamaliel, after stating, as above, the need to work for the community, continues[15] with, 'Be cautious in your dealings with the government, for they do not make advances to a man except in their own interest. They seem like friends at the time when it is advantageous for them, but they do not stand by man when he is in trouble.' The idea of working with a community 'for the sake of Heaven' is also expressed, in slightly different form, in a saying[16] attributed to R Johanan the sandalmaker: 'Every assembly [*kenesiah*] which is for the sake of Heaven will be established and that which is not for the sake of Heaven will not be established.' In all probability, the reference here is not to the Jewish community as a whole but to a meeting arranged for communal purposes, where there is the danger of personal interest and the lust for power gaining the upper hand. An anonymous saying in *Avot*[17] has it:

Everyone who makes many virtuous, no sin will result from his actions. But everyone who makes many sin, no opportunity will be given to him to repent. Moses was virtuous himself and he made the many virtuous, and their virtue is ascribed to him, as it is said: 'He executed the righteousness of the Lord and his judgement with Israel' (Deuteronomy 33:21). Jeroboam the son of Nebat sinned and caused the many to sin; the sin of the many is ascribed to him, as it is said: 'The sin of Jeroboam who sinned and made Israel sin.' (Kings 14:16)

Especially when the community is in trouble – from famine, for example – it is necessary for the individual to pray with them for their deliverance and to associate himself with them even if he himself faces no danger. The verse 'And unto Joseph were born two sons before the year of famine came' (Genesis 41:50), is made to yield the teaching that one must refrain from conjugal relations in years of famine. However, it is said, people who have no children may perform their marital duty even in years of famine;[18] a good example of the way in which the Rabbis tried to bring about the correct balance between the individual and the community to which he belongs and in whose distress he must share. In the same Talmudic passage[19] we read:

Our Rabbis have taught: If an individual separates himself from the community when the latter is in distress, the two ministering angels that accompany every man, place their hands upon his head and say, such and such a man has separated himself from the community, let him not live to witness the comfort of the community. Another teaching has it: When the community is in distress a man should not say, I will go home, eat and drink, and peace will be on my soul. If he does, Scripture says of him: 'And behold joy and gladness, slaying oxen and killing sheep, eating flesh and drinking wine – "let us eat and drink, for tomorrow we shall die"' (Isaiah 22:13). Now, what are the words which follow this verse? 'And the Lord of hosts revealed Himself in mine ears, surely this iniquity shall not be expiated by you till ye die'... A man should therefore afflict himself with the community, for thus we find that Moses afflicted himself out of sympathy with the community, as it is said: 'But Moses' hands were heavy and they took a stone and put it under him, and he sat thereon' (Exodus 17:12). Now did not Moses have a cushion or a pillow to sit upon? But Moses said: 'since Israel is in trouble, I shall share in their distress'.

In a particularly virulent denunciation it is said[20] that, among other extreme sinners, whose who have abandoned the ways of the community, those who 'spread their terror in the land of the living' (based on Ezekiel 32:2) and those who sin and make others to sin, like Jeroboam son of Nebat and his fellows, will go down to Gehinnom and be punished there for all generations. The expression 'those who spread their terror in the land of the living' is explained as a communal leader who makes himself unduly feared not for the sake of Heaven. There are echoes in this of the twin dangers that must often have faced the Jewish community. On the other hand, there were those who refused to have anything to do with the community but, on the other hand, there were those who were only too anxious to lead the community in order to enjoy dominion over others.

The supremacy of the community is to be seen in the principle laid down in Rabbinic law that no law can be imposed on the community unless a majority of its members can abide by it. After the destruction of the Temple, for instance, it was ruled that while some mourning rites had to be imposed these had to be restricted, otherwise the law would be too much of a burden on the community.[21] Again, after the destruction of the Temple and the devastations caused by the wars against Rome, it was said that all cattle breeding should be forbidden because of the harm the cattle could cause to the newly planted shoots. Nevertheless, only small cattle were placed under the prohibition since it was not too difficult to import these. To ban large cattle would have been to impose a rule on the community which the majority of their members could not accept.[22]

Members of a particular community were expected to contribute financially to the upkeep of the communal institutions, usually by a system of taxation but, in addition, by voluntary contributions.[23] In many synagogues, individual members became permanent seat-holders, paying for the privilege. In Temple times, of course, donations for the upkeep of the Temple were made and free-will offerings brought in addition to the obligatory sacrifices.[24] The prayer for the congregation in the traditional prayer book[25] reads:

> May He who blessed our fathers, Abraham, Isaac and Jacob, bless all this holy congregation, together with all other holy congregations: them, their wives, their sons and daughters, and all that belong to them; those also who establish synagogues for prayer, and those who enter therein to pray; those who give the lamps for lighting, wine for Kiddush and Habdalah, bread to the wayfarers, and charity to the poor, and all such as occupy themselves in faithfulness with the wants of the congregation.

Human nature being what it is, many generous donors wished to record their gifts in the form of a plaque or inscription recording that *A* had given this or that object to the synagogue. To this day such a name can be seen on the walls of the old synagogue in Cordoba and it appears to have been the regular practice in mediaeval Spanish synagogues. An early reference to the practice is found in the Responsa collection of the Rabbi of Barcelona, Solomon ibn Adret (*c*. 1235–*c* 1310), the *Rashba*,[26] who first states the question and then gives his reply:

Question. 'You ask: Reuben owned a house adjacent to the synagogue which, after some discussion with the members, he wished to donate for the enlargement of the synagogue. They came to an agreement and it was done. But now Reuben wishes his name to be recorded at the entrance to the synagogue so that his name will be remembered. Some members of the synagogue object to it. Please inform me if they have a right to object.'
Reply. 'I cannot see how the members of the community can or should object for a number of reasons. For when someone dedicates to Heaven that which belongs to him or builds something, paying for it himself, who can prevent him having his name recorded since no one has a right to prevent another from making any stipulation he wishes when donating such gifts. Furthermore, it is the custom to do it in that community and we [in Barcelona] also record the names of donors on the walls of the synagogue.'

The *Rashba* proceeds to quote from the sources that it is right and proper to acknowledge those who carry out good deeds. The Torah records it when Reuben saved Joseph (Genesis 37:21) and when Boaz helped Ruth (Ruth 2:14). The Talmud[27] tells of how Jose b. Joezer consecrated a loft full of denarii and his son sold to the Temple a pearl of the value of thirteen lofts of denarii but they only had seven so the son donated the remainder to the Temple and they recorded: 'Joseph b. Joezer brought in one but his son brought in six', from which it can be seen that it was the practice to write down the amounts given to the Temple and the names of the donors. Isserles in his gloss to the *Shulḥan 'Arukh*[28] states that a man who gives generously to a good cause should not boast of his good deed. 'Nevertheless', Isserles continues, 'one who makes a donation to a charitable cause may have his name recorded and it will be a remembrance for him and it is good to do this.' Isserles, in the sixteenth century, bases his opinion on the *Rashba* and evidently makes a distinction between boasting of the good deed, of which he disapproves, and having a record as a 'remembrance', of which he is in favour.[29]

From Talmudic times, every Jewish community had its system of poor relief[30] for which the members were taxed. In addition there were, of course, voluntary contributions. In the Bible there is an elaborate system of tithing and this was extended later to a tithe on all wealth, according to which a tenth of one's annual income has to be set aside for charitable purposes.[31] A pious individual would often give more than a tenth but the Talmud records[32] that, after the destruction of the Temple, the Rabbis decreed at the Synod of Usha that none should give more than a fifth. This was no doubt a measure against communal impoverishment after the decline of the economy in Palestine at that time, but the rule was recorded in the later Codes.[33] Yet there are instances of people giving away more than a fifth in times of great communal distress. R Shneor Zalman of Liady, for instance, urges his followers to disregard the rule since, he argues, the rule cannot apply where people are starving and must be helped to survive.[34]

Great care must be taken when giving charity not to humiliate the poor man who is the recipient. Maimonides' eight degrees of charity,[35] based on Talmudic sources, became the ideal in this matter of individual care for the poor:

There are eight degrees of charity one higher than the other. The highest degree of all is when one strengthens the hand of an Israelite who faces poverty, giving him a gift or a loan or entering into a business partnership with him or giving him a job in order to strengthen his hand and to prevent him becoming an object of charity... A lesser degree is where one gives charity to the poor but neither the giver nor the receiver knows of the other... A lesser degree is where the giver knows to whom he has given but the poor man does not know to whom he is indebted... Less than this is where the poor man knows to whom he is indebted but the giver does not know to whom he has given... Less than this is where the giver gives money directly to the poor man but without having to be asked for it. Less than this is where he gives after the poor man has asked him to do so. Less than this is where he gives the poor man less than he should but with a cheerful countenance. Less than this is where the giver is glum.

The way in which the life of the individual is linked to the community in Judaism can be seen particularly in the matter of prayer. While the many prayers in the Bible are individual prayers, summoned forth by particular circumstances,[36] Rabbinic Judaism introduced the idea of communal prayer – *tefillah be-tzibbur*[37] – as of supreme value. Menahem Meiri of Perpignan[38] (thirteenth century) in his typical demythologizing way of interpreting Talmudic sayings, comments as follows on the Talmudic statement[39] that prayer in a quorum of ten in the synagogue causes the Shekhinah to be present:

Whenever a man is able to recite his prayers in the synagogue he should do so since there proper concentration of the heart can be achieved. The Rabbis laid down a great rule: Communal prayer has especial value and whenever ten pray in the synagogue the Shekhinah is present.

According to this teacher, the individual ought ideally to pray in the synagogue together with the community because of its psychological effect. An individual is better able to concentrate on the prayers if the atmosphere is conducive to prayer both because of the sacredness of the place and because others are engaged in the same activity.

The Talmudic Rabbis often speak of the high value of communal prayer in the synagogue. 'One who has a synagogue in his town but does not enter therein to pray is called a bad neighbour [i.e. of God]'[40] is a typical Talmudic saying. While an individual can recite the statutory prayers on his own, there are some prayers (those described as 'prayers of sanctification') which can be recited only when a quorum of ten is present.[41] But, from the way Maimonides formulates it, it appears that, apart from the sanctification prayers, it is not so much an obligation to pray together with the congregation as an act of special piety.[42] Maimonides writes:[43]

> Communal prayer is always hearkened to and even if there are sinners among them the Holy One, blessed be He, does not reject the prayers of the many. Consequently, a man should associate himself with the community and he should not recite prayers in private whenever he is able to recite them together with the community.

Others see communal prayer as a definite obligation and in Jewish communities everywhere, nowadays, it is so seen.

In the literature of Jewish piety various reasons are given for the supremacy of communal over private prayer in addition to the greater psychological effect noted by Meiri. A mystical reason given by the Zohar[44] is that prayers offered in private do not ascend to God until the one who offers them has first been examined to see whether or not he is worthy for his prayers to be accepted, whereas communal prayers ascend immediately without any prior investigation. A variation of this is given by R Hayyim of Volozhyn with particular attention to what this early nineteenth-century author considers to be the spiritual decline of the age. Even in former ages, public prayer was superior to private but the latter could also be undertaken without risk. But, 'nowadays', it is extremely hazardous to undertake private prayer, for one who does so is trying, in effect, to bring about the aims of prayer life on his own and for this the kind of concentration required is beyond the reach of men in these weak generations. It is quite otherwise when people pray together. Then far less is demanded of the individual, supported as he is by his fellow worshippers.[45]

A full-scale treatment of the subject is provided in Judah Halevi's *Kuzari*.[46] In the dialogue, on which the book is based, between the King of the Khazars and the Jewish sage, the king asks, would it not be better if everyone read his prayers for himself? Would not this result in greater purity of thought and more intense concentration? The sage, in reply, lists the advantages of communal prayer. An individual, praying on his own, may pray for harm to come to others but a community will never pray for harm to come to one of its members. Furthermore, an individual may make mistakes in his mouthing of the prayers but when people pray together they make up for one another's shortcomings.

The idea, mentioned by Maimonides and implied by Halevi, that the sinners in a congregation are assisted by the prayers of the righteous, is found in the Talmud but there it is further said that in times of distress, such as when the community is praying for rain on a public fast day, it is essential to have the sinners as members of the community. Just as galbanum, which has, on its own, an unpleasant odour, had to be mixed with the other, sweet-smelling, ingredients when the incense was prepared for Temple use, so, too, the sinners are an integral part of the community.[47] The Jewish community, in other words, is not a community of saints. It is made up of many diverse individuals with a common aim despite the fact that many of them fall short of it in their daily lives. In Jewish folk language the word for community – *tzibbur* – is said to be the initial letters of *tzaddikim* ('righteous') *benonim* ('average persons'), *resha'im* ('wicked').[48] It takes all sorts to make a Jewish community as it takes all sorts to make a world.

In another area, too, there are tensions between the individual and the community. This is the important area of study of the Torah. While strong disapproval is expressed in the Talmud of those who study on their own,[49] this did not mean that individual scholars were obliged to conform to any standard norm, except, naturally, when it came to practical decision making where the majority view prevailed.[50] On the contrary, so far as theoretical learning and debate were concerned, the whole of the Talmud and of subsequent Jewish learning consists of arguments by individuals defending, often with vehemence, their own opinions.[51] This may be behind the saying that a scholar is allowed to forgo the honour due to him. And when it is objected that the Torah is not his, that he should have the right to waive the honour due to it, the reply is given, 'Verily, the

Torah is *his*.'[52] Throughout the history of Jewish learning there are not only many different branches of study but within each of these there has been much room for the exercise of individual disposition and temperament. A Talmudic saying has it that a man can only study a subject to which his heart draws him.[53] With the invention of printing and the resulting very wide dissemination of books, private study came into its own and it was held by many scholars that the authors of the books were 'study companions'.[54]

This leads to a consideration of how far individual dissent is tolerated in the Jewish tradition. It cannot be denied that Jewish communities exercised restraint on their dissidents by means of the *ḥerem* and, sometimes, by coercion. The statement in the Talmud[55] that the Court can punish offenders even where there are no strictly legal grounds for so doing, 'where the generation needs it', resulted, especially in the mediaeval Spanish communities, in the strictest control by the Rabbis and communal leaders of non-conformism, and the case of Spinoza hardly requires to be mentioned. But all this took place in more or less closed communities where the game was generally played according to the rules. The banning of unconventional or heretical views has no meaning in the open and pluralistic Jewish society that is the norm in contemporary Jewish life. Even Orthodox Rabbis of note have taught that the harsh treatment meted out, at least theoretically, in the traditional sources no longer applies.[56] Religious tolerance undoubtedly belongs to Western society but, after the Emancipation, the majority of Jews belong in that society.

CHAPTER 7

God and the soul

The relationship between the individual and God can be considered from two points of view. In Jewish teaching the soul of each individual is unique, with its own special relationship with God, and each individual has to employ his body in giving expression to this relationship. In this chapter the soul relationship with God is examined, the next chapter the body relationship. In both chapters it is the individual *qua* individual that is considered apart from the relationship of the individual to God as a member of the Jewish people.

Generally in the Jewish tradition the individual soul is totally distinct from God, who creates the soul as something quite other than He. But there is to be found, among some of the Jewish mystics, the astonishing idea of the 'divine spark' in man, according to which, ultimately, there is something in the human soul, or, at least, in the Jewish soul, that is itself indistinct from God. It is this startling doctrine that we must here examine.

The belief that there is a special mystical 'spark' in every human breast can be traced back, in Western mysticism, at least to Jerome in the fourth century. Both Bonaventura and Bernard of Clairvaux speak of this mystical organ; the latter called it *scintillula*, a small spark of the soul,[1] and, speaking of the nearness of God, said: 'Angels and archangels are within us, but He is more truly our own who is not only *with us* but *in us*.'[2] However, both these mystics are anxious to prevent an identification of this mystical spark with the divine. Eckhart, on the other hand, embraces the identification, calling the spark, among other endearing names, *das Kleidhaus Gottes*,[3] 'the house in which God attires Himself'. This and other pantheistic tendencies in Eckhart's thought were condemned in the papal Bull of 1529.[4]

In Eastern mysticism the identification of the mystical spark with the divine is frequent. In the Upanishads *Atman* is *Brahman*; the soul of man is identical with the universal principle, *tat tvam asi*, 'That art thou'. 'This my spirit within my heart is greater than the earth, greater than the sky, greater than the heavens, greater than all worlds. The all-working, all-wishing, all-smelling, all-tasting one, that embraces the universe, that is silent, untroubled – that is the spirit within my heart, that is Brahman. Thereunto, when I go hence, shall I attain. Who knoweth this, he, sooth, hath no more doubts.'[5] Sankara (d. 820), the famous Hindu mystic, describes the identification in these terms:

That same highest Brahman constitutes – as we know from such passages as 'That art thou' – the real nature of the individual soul, while its second nature, i.e. that aspect of it which depends on fictitious limiting conditions, is not its real nature... But when, after disregarding the aggregate of body, sense-organs and mind, it arrives, by means of Scripture, at the knowledge that it is not itself that aggregate, that it does not form part of transmigratory existence, but is the True, the Realm, the Self, whose nature is pure intelligence; then knowing itself to be of the nature of unchangeable, eternal Cognition, it lifts itself above the main conceit of being one with this body, and itself becomes the Self, whose nature is unchangeing, eternal Cognition.[6]

In Islamic mysticism, the idea appears, from Hallaj, with his *Ana'l-Ḥaqq*, 'I am the Truth (which is God)', to Jalal-ud-din Rumi's proclamation that the soul's love of God is God's love of the soul, and that in loving the soul God loves Himself, for He draws home to Himself that which is in its essence divine.[7] In an ode this poet says:[8]

O my soul, I searched from end to end: I saw
in thee naught but the Beloved:
Call me not infidel, O my soul, if I say that
thou thyself art He.

It is generally asserted that in every version of Judaism the distance between God and man is so vast that ideas such as the preceding can have no place in the Jewish faith. Salo Baron,[9] for instance, makes the following generalization:

But while Muslim fatalism tended to reduce greatly the distance between the Creator and the universe or man created by him, thus opening the road to unrestrictedly pantheistic identification, Jews (even the Sufis among them) had retained enough of their traditional awe before the divine

Holiness and its inherent transcendence to draw a sharp line of demarcation between them...But in their most daring dialogues and visions they never forgot the chasm which separated the Infinite from all His creatures, even those belonging to the highest emanations, which alone the 'Descenders of the Chariot' dared to approach. In the ultimate sense, even these mystics resigned themselves in their diverse ways, to the acceptance of the inscrutable tortuousness of the divine guidance of man and history. Individually, too, they sought mere communion, not actual union, with the Deity.

It should be clear that Baron is correct only if his observation is limited to the *Merkavah* ('Chariot') mysticism with which he deals. The categorical statement that Judaism, in any of its forms, knows nothing of the identification of the 'divine spark' with the divine can be maintained only by ignoring a considerable portion of the evidence now to be adduced. Consequently, R. C. Zaehner's remarks are true only of 'normative' Judaism, not of Judaism in all its manifestations:

It can be maintained that the strictly monotheistic religions do not naturally lend themselves to mysticism: and there is much to be said for this view...Judaism, on its side, never developed a mystical tradition comparable to that of the other great religions because it held that union with a transcendental God who manifests himself in history could not be possible to a finite creature.[10]

Zaehner quotes Scholem[11] as his authority: 'The Creator and His creatures remain apart, and nowhere is an attempt made to bridge the gap between them or to blur the distinction.' But Scholem is speaking of 'Chariot' mysticism and if his remarks are intended to apply to every type of Jewish mysticism his view is contradicted by the evidence to be adduced.

David Baumgardt[12] is on surer ground when remarking on the 'divine spark' idea:

The way in which similar ideas about an inner well of religious life emerges in movements with hardly any contact with Christian religious thought, may be inferred from the sayings of the founder of the Habad Society, or Lubavitcher Hasidim, Shneur Zalman of Ladi in Lithuania (1745–1813),[13] who was called the 'Rav of Reussen' or 'alter Rebbe' (the old Rebbi). He taught in his *Sefer Tanya* that in every Jewish soul there is a spark of divinity (according to popular Jewish thought 'a small point of Jewish faith' [*dos pintele Yid*] by which religious Jewishness can, on principle, always be rekindled, no matter how hidden it may be or how dead it may appear to the eye of the observer).

We shall see that Baumgardt is certainly right in finding this idea in *Ḥabad*. But it has its antecedents in earlier Jewish thought. It is our present purpose to consider the doctrine of the 'divine spark' in the form it assumes in a number of important Jewish sources and to demonstrate that its prominence in *Ḥabad* comes at the end of a long process.

It is hardly necessary to state that there is no hint of the idea in the Bible. The verse, 'Then the Lord God formed man of the dust of the ground, and breathed into his nostrils the breath of life' (Genesis 2:7), though used as a proof-text for the notion of the 'divine spark', by Philo and others, really means no more than that God blew the spirit into Adam.[14] 'The spirit of man is the candle of the Lord' (Proverbs 20:27) means, of course, a candle *kindled* by the Lord. 'And the dust returneth to the earth as it was, and the spirit returneth unto God who gave it' (Ecclesiastes 12:7) similarly means no more than that God *gave* man his soul, not that the soul is part of God.

Philo, writing at the beginning of the first century CE, was the first Jew, so far as we know, to teach that there is something divine in the human soul:

For the essence or substance of that other soul is divine spirit, as truth vouched for by Moses especially, who in his story of the creation says that God breathed a breath of life upon the first man, the founder of our race, into the lordliest part of the body, the face, where the senses are stationed like bodyguards to the great king, the mind. And clearly what was then thus breathed was ethereal spirit, even an effulgence of the blessed, thrice blessed nature of the Godhead.[15]

Philo reverts to the idea of the soul as an 'effulgence of the blessed nature of the Godhead' in a number of passages in his works. Thus in his comment on Genesis 2:7 he says:[16]

'Breathed into', we note, is equivalent to 'inspired' or 'besouled' the soulless, for God forbid that we should be infected with such monstrous folly as to think that God employs for inbreathing organs such as mouth and nostrils; for God is not only not in the form of a man, but belongs to no class or kind. Yet the expression clearly brings out something that accords with nature. For it implies of necessity three things, that which inbreathes, that which receives, that which is inbreathed: that which inbreathes is God, that which receives is the mind, that which is inbreathed is the spirit or breath. What, then, do we infer from these premisses? A union of the three comes about, as God projects the power that proceeds from Himself through the mediant breath till it reaches the subject. And for what purpose save that we may obtain a conception of Him? For how could the soul have conceived of God, had He not breathed into it and mightily laid hold of it? For the mind of man would never have ventured to soar so high as to grasp the nature of God, had not God Himself drawn it up to Himself, so far as it was possible that the mind of man should be drawn up, and stamped it with the impress of the powers that are within the scope of its understanding.

Thus, according to Philo, the human mind would be incapable of knowing God were it not that God had permitted the abyss to be crossed by infusing the mind with something of Himself. Elsewhere[17] Philo states that the gift of a divine part of the soul to Adam is shared by his descendants, albeit in fainter form. Every man, he says, in respect of his mind, is allied to the divine Reason, having come into being as a copy or fragment or ray of that blessed nature. In the later literature the 'divine spark' is frequently limited to Israel. In Philo the more universalistic tendency prevails. All Adam's descendants share in his nature and have something of the divine within them.

If we turn to the Rabbinic literature[18] we find references to the purity of the soul[19] and its heavenly origin.[20] Just as the woman of royal lineage who marries a villager is never satisfied with all that her husband provides because she is accustomed to life in the royal palace, so the soul's immortal longings are never satisfied because it derives from 'those above' (*ha-'elyonim*).[21] In a famous passage[22] it is stated that the soul resembles God in that it is invisible, it sustains the body as God sustains the world, it is pure, it fills the body as God fills the world, and, like God, it dwells in the innermost chambers. In all this there is not the slightest hint at any identification of the soul with God. The nearest to such identification in the whole of the Rabbinic literature is the saying of R Eleazer (third century)[23] that a man should consider himself as if the Holy One dwells within him; but even if this is what R Eleazer really means (and this is by no means certain[24]), it is clear from the context that he is simply stating in picturesque fashion the need for man to take good care of himself, since his bodily needs are also God-given. It would be exceedingly precarious to deduce from this isolated saying that there are Rabbinic echoes of the Philonic idea.

Nor is there any clear attempt at the identification of the soul and God in the classical mediaeval philosophers. These agree that the soul is not material, and the Aristotelian threefold division of the soul into vegetative, animal and rational is frequently found. Under the influence of the Arabic Aristotelians the doctrine of the Active Intellect was adopted by thinkers like Abraham Ibn Da'ud, Maimonides, Gersonides and Crescas. By means of the Active Intellect, which emanates from God, man can gain an acquired intellect, through the exercise of his mind in study and comprehension of metaphysical truth. This alone is the immortal part of man.[25] All this has little to do with the doctrine that there is a divine spark hidden in the recesses of the human psyche. However, a Neo-Platonist like Gabirol (d. 1058) can refer to the soul as a pure radiance from God's glory:[26]

> Who can contain Thy might when from the abundance
> of Thy glory Thou didst create a pure
> radiance, hewn from the quarry of the Rock,
> and dug from the mine of Purity?
> And on it Thou didst set a spirit of wisdom, and
> Thou didst call it the Soul.
> Thou didst fashion it from the flames of fire of
> the Intelligence, and its spirit is as a fire
> burning in it.
> Thou didst send it into the body to serve it...

It is in the teaching of the Kabbalah, with its strong Neo-Platonic influences, that the doctrine of the 'divine spark' comes into full prominence in Jewish thought. The Zoharic teachings on the nature of the soul are exceedingly complex,[27] but at least in one passage[28] it is clearly stated that the highest part of the soul – *neshamah* – comes from the Sefirotic realm, from the 'body' of *Adam Kadmon*, Primordial Man, the world of the *Sefirot*, emanating from *En Sof*, the Infinite – God as He is in Himself:

> Rabbi Judah began his discourse by quoting the verse, 'Let every soul praise the Lord' (Psalm 150:6). We have been taught that all souls are derived from that Holy Body and they animate human beings. From which place are they derived? From the place that is called *Yah*. Which place is that? Said Rabbi Judah, It is written: 'How manifold are Thy works, O Lord. In wisdom hast Thou made them all' (Psalm 104:24). We have been taught that all things are contained in that wisdom the spring of which flows into thirty-two paths; all things above and below are contained within it.

In the Zoharic scheme the highest *Sefirot* are: *Keter*, 'Crown', the divine Will; *Ḥokhmah*, the divine Wisdom; and *Binah*, the divine Understanding. In the above passage the soul is said to derive ultimately from the divine Wisdom. This means much more than that God in His Wisdom created the soul. The *Sefirah* of Wisdom is in Zoharic thought an aspect of the Deity. Consequently, the soul comes from God Himself. In other Zoharic sources it is suggested that the soul comes from the *Sefirah* of Understanding.[29] The author of the Zohar, remarks Gershom Scholem,[30] on the whole holds the view that only the *nefesh*, the natural soul, is capable of sin. The *neshamah*, the spark of the divine in man, is beyond sin. Indeed, Moses de Leon, identified with good reason by Scholem as the author of the Zohar, discusses in other works of his how it is possible for the soul to suffer in Hell since *neshamah* is substantially the same as God.

Nahmanides (1195–1270), in his Commentary to the Pentateuch, on the verse, 'Then the Lord God formed man of the dust of the ground, and breathed into his nostrils the breath of life; and man became a living soul' (Genesis 2:7), gives an interpretation in the spirit of the Kabbalah, which bears remarkable affinities with Philo's interpretation of the same verse. Nahmanides observes[31] that the verse provides us with a hint of the soul's most elevated nature by using the complete divine name – 'the Lord God'. By stating that God 'breathed' the soul 'into his nostrils' the verse teaches that the soul has its origin neither in the four elements nor as an emanation from the disembodied intelligences, the angels, but from the very 'mouth' of God. Nahmanides quotes for his purpose, 'Out of His mouth cometh knowledge and discernment' (Proverbs 2:6). The soul is thus a spirit which comes from God Himself. For when one blows into the face of another it is of his own breath which he blows.[32] Quoting 'But it is a spirit in man and the breath of the Almighty that giveth them understanding' (Job 32:8), Nahmanides refers to the Kabbalistic doctrine that the soul comes from the divine Understanding, i.e. from the *Sefirah* of that name. He then goes on to discuss the different parts of the soul under the conventional mediaeval categories. At all events, according to this author, there is a portion of the divine in the soul of man.

Nahmanides was the first Bible commentator to make use of the Kabbalah for exegetical purposes. In this he was followed by Bahya Ibn Asher (d. 1340) of Saragossa. After a lengthy exposition of the different views on the nature of the soul held by the philosophers,

Bahya[33] turns, in his comment to the *locus classicus* on the question, Genesis 2:7, to the views of the Kabbalah:

That the soul, after its departure from the body, is immortal is stated in this verse which calls it the 'soul of life' (*nishmat ḥayyim*), namely, a soul hewn out of the Source of life, for the soul is hewn out of the Source of the divine Wisdom... Solomon says: 'Man's pre-eminence above the beast is nothing' (Ecclesiastes 3:19). He states that the pre—eminence of man over the beast is by virtue of that which is called 'Nothing', that is to say, by virtue of man's rational soul which derives from Wisdom... Hence the verse speaks of God as breathing into his nostrils that wc might understand the foundation of the soul and its most elevated state, since it emanates from the Holy Spirit. It is for this reason that the soul is compared to the Holy One, blessed be He, in five matters[34]... The Sage observes: 'Know yourselves and you will know God.'[35]

The ideas of both Nahmanides and Bahya were drawn upon by Manasseh ben Israel (d. 1657) in his treatise on the soul.[36] Referring to the verse quoted by the previous authors he observes[37] that this calls attention to the spiritual and elevated nature of the soul, which emanates from the Holy Spirit – the very words used by Bahya. It is as if 'the Holy One, blessed be He, as it were, touched the formless lump of Adam and blew the soul into it, thereby imparting to man some of the divine wisdom'. The souls of all other animals were created together with their bodies, but man's soul, being divine, was infused into him after his body had been created from the dust. Those who 'prepare savouries' (i.e. rather fanciful comments to Scripture) are quoted by the author in pointing out that the letters of the word for soul, *neshamah*, are largely the same as those in the word for heaven, *shamayim*, to hint at the divine original of the soul.

The Kabbalist Hayyim Vital (1545–1620) elaborates on the theme of the divine soul in his *Sha'arey Kedushah*,[38] 'Gates of Holiness'. The true man, states Vital, is not the body, for this is known in Scripture as the 'flesh of man'. The soul is the real man, using the body as its garment. At death the soul divests itself of the coarse garment of the body to become clothed with pure, refined, spiritual vestments. As a result of Adam's sin there came about a mixture of good and evil in all things so that even the divine soul, hewn from the four divine elements represented by the four letters of the Tetragrammaton, became surrounded by an evil soul, deriving from the forces of impurity and known as the Evil Inclination. The limbs of the physical body are garments to the spiritual 'limbs' of the unclean soul and these are, in turn, garments to the 'limbs' of the pure soul, the true man. When man uses his bodily limbs for sin he adds fuel to the forces of the impure soul. When he uses them to perform good deeds these nourish and sustain the divine soul, enabling it to get the upper hand of the unclean soul. In later parts of the work[39] Vital describes in detail the whole scheme by which man's psychic nature is linked to the 'upper worlds'. One passage in particular[40] deserves passing notice:

The soul's greatness has been described, for it is a great light born of the light of the *Sefirot* themselves, without any intermediary. This is the meaning of, 'Ye are children of the Lord your God' (Deuteronomy 14:1) for they are in the category of a son who is completely attached to the father from whom he is descended. This is the mystery behind the saying that the Patriarchs are the Heavenly Chariot[41] to the light of the *Sefirot* which rides above them without the mediation of any other light... This is the meaning of the verse, 'For as the girdle cleaveth to the loins of a man, so have I caused to cleave unto Me the whole house of Israel' (Jeremiah 13:11).

It will be seen that for Vital, as for the majority of the Kabbalists, the elevated role of divine kinship is reserved for Israel, and is really based on the notion that Israel on earth mirrors the heavenly pattern.

Vital was the disciple of the famous Safed Kabbalist Isaac Luria (1534–72). An earlier mystic of the Safed mystical school was Moses Cordovero[42] (1522–70). Elijah de Vidas, Cordovero's pupil, published his own *Reshit Ḥokhmah*[43] ('Beginning of Wisdom') as an ethical guide for the mystical adept, in the spirit of his master. Here the doctrine of the divine spark in man is treated in elaborate detail[44] and, like much of de Vidas' work, owes a great deal to Cordovero. Claiming that his ideas are based on the Zohar,[45] though it is only through considerable homiletical ingenuity that the passage quoted can be made to yield the thought, de Vidas states that an actual spark (*nitzutz*) of the Holy One, blessed be He, and his Shekhinah is contained within man.

De Vidas writes, 'Souls are flaming threads drawn down below from on high, their vitality stemming constantly from their Source.' In his view death is caused by God drawing up to Himself the thread by which the soul is bound to Him, just as the scent of an apple is drawn away when one smells its fragrance. This is why Scripture says, 'For the portion of the Lord is His people, Jacob the lot of His inheritance' (Deuteronomy 32:9). The soul of an Israelite is an actual portion of the Deity (taking the word 'portion' not in the sense of a part *belonging* to God but to mean a part *of* God). This does not mean, however, that there is any kind of separateness or division in God but rather that the source of the soul on high is a part of God. Souls inhabiting individual bodies are naturally separate entities but in their source in God they are one with Him. 'For the portion of the Lord is His people' can be read as 'For the portion of the Lord is with Him' (*'immo* for *'ammo*); i.e. God's portion of the soul, the part that is divine, is 'with' Him as part of His being with its branches here below. Hence the verse speaks, too, of Jacob as the 'rope' (*ḥevel* can mean 'rope' as well as 'lot') of His inheritance, for the soul and God are united like the strands of which a rope is composed. Furthermore, the illustration of a rope is given to denote that the soul, even after its descent into the body, is still attached to God, so that one end of the 'rope' is in God's hands while the other inhabits the body. 'The meaning of the love of God and "cleaving" to Him is that man attaches himself to God by means of this link, binding himself to the root of his soul which is attached to God, blessed be He.' Just as man's soul loves his body to which it is joined and the body the soul as the source of its life, so should man love God with whom his soul is united.

Shabbetai Sheftel Horowitz the Elder (d. 1619) flourished in Prague and was the author of the famous Kabbalistic book *Shefa' Tal*.[46] At the beginning of the work[47] Horowitz writes:

It is known that the souls of the people of Israel are 'a portion of God from above'[48] (Job 31:2). The verse, 'For the portion of the Lord is His people' (Deuteronomy 32:9) hints at this. The term 'portion' is to be taken literally. A portion separated from some thing is in every way like the thing from which it has been taken, the thing being the whole and the total, which is naturally greater than the part separated thereof. But in essence the whole and the part are identical. In the same way there is no difference or distinction between the soul and God, may He be exalted and may His name be exalted, except that God, may He be exalted and His name exalted, is the whole. He is the all-embracing light, the infinite, unending, great light, whereas the soul is a portion and a spark separated from the great light, blessed be He and blessed be His name. As King Solomon, on whom be peace, says, 'The spirit of man is the candle of the Lord' (Proverbs 20:27). He means to say that man's soul is a candle, a spark deriving from God's light. He takes particular care to speak of the 'candle [*ner*] of the Lord' rather than the 'light of the Lord' in order to hint at the truth that all three degrees of *nefesh*, *ruaḥ* and *neshamah* in the soul are a portion and a spark of God's light. This is hinted at by the use of the expression the '*ner* of God' since the word '*ner*' has the initial letters of *nefesh* and *ruaḥ*.[49] The meaning is that *nefesh*, *ruaḥ* and *neshamah*, the three degrees of the soul, are all holy sparks which come from God's light. Hence the verse says, 'The *neshamah* of man is the *ner* of God.'

It can be seen that Horowitz draws almost entirely on his predecessors. He is extraordinary only in giving such prominence to the doctrine of the divine spark, placing it at the beginning of his lengthy treatise.

Horowitz was not unaware of the offence-giving nature of his contention. No sooner had he written this first paragraph than he added a cautionary note to the reader, warning him not to jump to conclusions on this extremely complex and difficult theme, one which, if incorrectly grasped, can seem to border on the blasphemous. This note reads:

O student of this work, be not astonished at this idea; for my master and teacher, Rabbi Moses Cordovero, has written even more than this in his holy *Pardes*,[50] Gate of *Hekhalot*, chapter 15, where he remarks, 'The Patriarchs are more elevated than the *Sefirot* for they are not "limbs" but are Divinity Itself in Its extension to creatures here below.' You see that he states explicitly that the Patriarchs are Divinity Itself. His words there and ours here will become perfectly intelligible to you when you reach the Gate of *nefesh*, *ruaḥ* and *neshamah* of this work. But I request the student to study this work in the order of its Gates and chapters, for each Gate and each chapter is the key, introduction and commentary to the Gates and chapters which follow it. Do not, therefore, permit your thoughts to skip immediately to the middle of this work, for this will be of no advantage to you. But if you study the work in the order we have mentioned the gates of light will be revealed to you without mental fatigue. However, as a preliminary thought and first postulate you may grasp this idea and understand it.

Horowitz's *Shefa' Tal* was no sooner off the press than it was widely acclaimed as a basic Kabbalistic text-book; but the fears of the author, that his notion of the divine character of the soul would give offence, were not unfounded. It appears, indeed, that so fierce were the protests it evoked that the author resolved to write a special work of defence against his critics. This little book, entitled *Nishmat Shabbetai ha-Levi*[51] ('The Soul of Shabbetai the Levite'), has the avowed aim of removing the misconceptions to which his formulation in the *Shefa' Tal* had given rise.

In the preface to his apology Horowitz states that the work deals with the mysteries of the holy soul which were revealed as a result of the difficulties raised by his sons, pupils, colleagues and teachers – a formidable list. The author claims, in his introduction, that mysteries still left concealed in his *Shefa' Tal* are now revealed so that the new work must be seen as an appendix to the earlier one. In fact, he remarks, he has now decided to give a new name to both books so that they can be treated as one. The new title, significantly enough, is *Galey Razaya* ('Revealer of Mysteries'). Horowitz further claims that, so far from being in any way original in his notions concerning the divine character of the soul, he has four great authorities – he calls them 'pillars' – on whom he relies; four earlier teachers of the highest renown who had taught the same truth. The first of these is none other than Moses himself, the second Rabbi Simeon b. Yohai, the traditionally reputed author of the Zohar, the third Nahmanides, the fourth Elijah de Vidas. The last two references are, of course, to the works we have mentioned previously. The book is divided into thirteen brief chapters, corresponding, the author informs us, to Maimonides' thirteen principles of the Jewish faith. They provide the reader with the basic principles of his psychic life.

In a special introduction to the 'Gates' of the treatise Horowitz proceeds to describe its purpose. His pupils and teachers, he observes, raised a 'tremendous objection' to the ideas on the nature of the soul contained in the *Shefa' Tal*. Sure of the value of the latter work, and perhaps being sensitive to the criticism it had evoked, he calls it a 'holy work, holy in all its parts, containing words of truth and uprightness, words of the living God, without any blemish'. The objections raised are then stated fairly. How can it be maintained that the soul is an actual part of God since this would mean that there are as many parts in God as the total number of Jewish souls, thus compromising traditional Jewish monotheism? All the Kabbalists agree that the Infinite – *En Sof* – has neither parts nor divisions. Furthermore, every Jewish child is taught to praise God for *creating* his soul, and the Rabbis speak of God *creating* the souls of Israel before the creation of the world. If the soul is *created* how can it be a portion of the Creator?[52] After a general introduction to the basic Kabbalistic principles regarding the relationship between *En Sof* (God as He is in Himself) and the *Sefirot* (God in the process of revealing Himself to others), the author begins his reply in Gate 4. He first calls attention to the note of warning issued at the beginning of the *Shefa' Tal*. Here he has reminded the reader of the dangers inherent in a superficial understanding of the notion of the divine spark. Denying emphatically that he is in any way recanting, he goes on to say that all along he had meant to say that the soul is a portion of the Sefirotic realm – God in His aspect of self-disclosure – not a portion of *En Sof*. *En Sof* is God as He is known to Himself alone. Of this aspect of Deity nothing whatsoever can be postulated. It is not mentioned in the Bible; It is utterly beyond all human comprehension; of It nothing can be said; It is entirely remote from the slightest attempt at comprehension. It follows that it is quite improper to speak of the soul as a portion of *En Sof*, since it is really improper to speak of *En Sof* at all. How then can one speak of a 'portion' of *En Sof*? *Shefa' Tal* denies that he had ever said that one could. Of the *Sefirot*, however, one can speak. Moreover these are ten in number. Hence there is division, for God as He reveals Himself to others has varying attributes and aspects. Consequently, it is quite proper to speak of the soul as a portion of the Sefirotic realm, for here there is division, and there can be no harm in extending the divisions to include the totality of souls.

This possibly lessens the difficulty. It does not abolish it. It is true that in the Kabbalah the distinction is made between *En Sof* and the *Sefirot*, but the Kabbalists felt bound to demonstrate that somehow there is no degeneration into dualism. Consequently, various illustrations are used by them to convey the thought that there is a basic unity of *En Sof* and the *Sefirot*. Among these illustrations are those of water poured into bottles of various colours, which partakes of the colour of the bottles without really suffering change; or of the human soul which is one and yet which possesses various characteristics; or of the multi-coloured flames proceeding from the one glowing coal. It follows that the doctrine of the divine spark – even if it comes from the Sefirotic realm – is still exceedingly bold. Hence, Horowitz, in the next three chapters, quotes his four 'pillars' in support of his radical viewpoint. Gate 5 gives an account of Nahmanides' view to which we have referred. In chapter 6 the second 'pillar', de Vidas, is quoted. Chapter 7 relies on the Zoharic passage quoted by de Vidas. As we have seen, the idea of the soul as a portion of God is far from explicit in this passage, although, since Horowitz now admits that he is thinking only of the Sefirotic realm, it is rather strange that he does not quote the Zoharic passages in which it is stated clearly that the soul comes either from the *Sefirah* of Wisdom or from that of Understanding. Finally, the strongest proof of all, Moses himself, is asserted to have referred to the doctrine in the Shema, Israel's declaration of faith: 'Hear O Israel, the Lord our God the Lord is One' (Deuteronomy 6:4). Horowitz is here somewhat obscure, but, if my reading of what he says is correct, he appears to interpret the verse with a boldness his critics would surely say does border on the blasphemous, in this way: 'Hear! Israel and the Lord our God are one Lord'. 'Israel', observes Horowitz, 'is united with God in the upper worlds.'

In the sources mentioned hitherto the doctrine of the divine spark in the soul is accepted, occasionally with qualifications, and it forms a more or less significant part in the spiritual outlook of the various authors. Nowhere, however, do we find such a highly developed metaphysical system based on the idea as we do in the writings of Shneor Zalman of Liady, mentioned above, the founder of the *Ḥabad* group in Hasidism. Shneor Zalman relies mainly on the Kabbalists of the Lurianic school, Hayyim Vital in particular.[53] Following Vital, Shneor Zalman speaks of the two souls which every Jew possesses. The first, the 'animal soul', is the vital force by which man lives. It is the source of his desires and his appetites. It is constantly at war with the 'divine soul', the portion of God within man. Here is Shneor Zalman's description of the divine soul:[54]

The second soul of Israel is an actual portion of God from above, as it is said, 'And he breathed into his nostrils the *neshamah* of life' (Genesis 2:7), and 'Thou didst breathe it into me.'[55] As the Zohar[56] comments, 'When one blows it is from himself that he blows', that is to say, from his most inward essence, for man ejects his most inner vitality when he blows powerfully. In the same way the souls of Israel ascended in God's thought, as it is written, 'Israel is My son, My first-born' (Exodus 4:22), 'Ye are children of the Lord your God' (Deuteronomy 14:1). This means that as the child derives from the brain of the father[57] so, as it were, the soul of every Jew is derived from God's thought and wisdom... the root of every *nefesh*, *ruaḥ* and *neshamah*, from the highest of all degrees to the lowest, in which the soul is clothed by the body of the ignorant man and the lowest of the low, derives from the Supernal Mind, the Supernal Wisdom, as in the illustration (if it is permitted to say this) of the child who stems from the brain of his father. Even the child's finger and toe nails are formed from the actual drop of semen which remains in the mother's womb for nine months, there descending from stage to stage until it changes so much that nails are formed, and yet, none the less, it is still bound to and united with, in marvellous fashion, its first essence when it was part of the brain of the father...

Prominent in *Ḥabad* thought is the idea of *bittul ha-yesh*, 'annihilation of the self'. From one point of view God is the only true Being – *yesh*, 'somethingness' – whereas all creatures, including man, are nothing – *ayin*, 'nothingness'. But from another point of view it is God who can be referred to as 'Nothing', because so far is

He from all human comprehension that of Him nothing can be said, whereas man can be referred to as *yesh*, 'that which is', that which is evident to the senses. Since the human soul is part of God it longs to return to its source in Him, but the human ego in its separateness creates a barrier between the soul and its source in God. In technical *Ḥabad* terms, man's *yesh*, his 'somethingness', acts as a screen before the divine 'Nothingness', *ayin*. The screen can be removed only by self-abnegation or self-annihilation. When man's ego is set at naught, when he attains to *bittul ha-yesh*, complete abandonment of his 'somethingness' as a being apart from God, he becomes *ayin*, 'nothingness', and he is then able to achieve contact with the 'Nothingness' that is God.[58] The veils of the senses and the ego are then stripped away and the soul in its naked 'nothingness' is in touch with its source in God. This is a tendency to be observed in much mystical thought, 'that the spark of the divine cannot be contained because it contains nothing but the All, that the vacuum is the richest fullness, the negative the highest degree of positivity'.[59] As the *Tao-teh King* puts it:[60]

> Thirty spokes meet together in a single hub.
> The waggon's usefulness depends on their
> nothingness [on the empty space between them]
> Clay is moulded into vessels;
> The vessels' utility depends on their
> nothingness.
> To build a house, holes are made in the walls
> for doors and windows;
> On their nothingness depends the usefulness of
> the house.
> Hence: Being yields possession, but Non-being
> utility.

It is well known that Hasidism found its strongest opponent in Elijah the Gaon of Vilna (1720–97). The opposition was on various grounds, not least the panentheistic viewpoint of Hasidism. The divine was seen by the adherents of the new sect in the most mundane of things. The famous disciple of the Gaon, Hayyim of Volozhyn (1740–1821), treats of Kabbalistic topics in his *Nefesh ha-Ḥayyim*.[61] The mystical ideas of this work are not very different from those of Shneor Zalman, whose writings were certainly familiar to Hayyim, but, for obvious reasons, greater caution is used in such an anti-Hasidic work. The author accepts, for instance, the idea of the divine spark in the soul but is far more qualified in his acceptance than Shneor Zalman. Hayyim admits that the 'essence' of the soul is divine, but he states that this 'essence' never enters the human body. Before Adam sinned he did, indeed, possess this 'essence' but it was taken from him when he ate of the fruit of the tree, remaining only in a state of suspension over him. Moses alone had the great merit of possessing the 'essence' of the divine soul while still in the body, hence he is called 'the man of God' (Deuteronomy 33:1). No other human being is in possession of it, but sparks flash from it over the heads of the saints, each according to the spiritual degree he occupies and his spiritual capacities.[62] Thus, for Hayyim, the divine spark has become a spark from the soul, not a spark of God, and even this is not a basic part of every man but is earned through saintly endeavours. A far cry this from the categorical statement of *Ḥabad*, that there is an actual portion of God in every Jewish soul.

If the opponents of Hasidism gave only a grudging recognition to the doctrine of the divine spark, the followers of Shneor Zalman of Liady furthered the powerful and influential *Ḥabad* movement with the doctrine as a central plank in its platform. One of the most remarkable mystical testimonies in the whole literature of mysticism is that of Shneor Zalman's son and successor, Dov Baer of Lubavitch (1775–1927). This work, entitled *Kunteros ha-Hitpa'alut* ('Tract on Ecstasy'), is in the form of a lengthy letter, sent by the master to his followers soon after his assumption of the leadership of the sect, offering them the guidance they had sought on the role of ecstasy in prayer.[63] Dov Baer teaches that two types of ecstasy are possible in prayer. There is the power of man's two souls, the 'animal' or 'natural' and the 'divine', in his prayer life. The force of the 'divine soul' is strong or weak according to man's nearness to God in his daily life and the amount of divine grace granted to him. Dov Baer describes the difference between the manifestations of the two souls in prayer as the difference between the 'essential' and the 'separate'. This means that an experience of the 'divine soul', though it is expressed through the normal channels of human will, thought and emotions, is, in reality, an experience of the divine by the divine, as it were. It is an 'essential' experience – divine essence responding to divine essence, the spark drawing near to the flame. An experience of the 'natural soul', on the other hand, through the channels of will, thought and emotions, is a 'separate' experience. It involves an encounter with the divine by something not itself divine. Ecstasy induced by the divine grace extending to awaken the 'divine soul' is referred to as 'serving the Lord with the soul', whereas ecstasy induced by contemplation through the channels of the 'natural soul' is called 'serving the Lord with the body'. The whole tract is a profound analysis of ecstatic states, spurious and authentic, but its detailed investigation does not belong here.[64]

We have tried to trace the doctrine of the divine spark in the soul from its beginnings in Philo, through the Kabbalists, and down to its significant place in the *Ḥabad* system. Admittedly, the doctrine is highly unconventional for Jewish religious thought, but for all the emphasis in normative Judaism on the impassable gulf between the individual soul and God, the daring idea did emerge in some circles that the abyss had been bridged.

CHAPTER 8

Does a person's body belong to God?

Some Halakhists have put forward the view that, while it is axiomatic in Jewish law that a man owns his property, whether real estate or movables,[1] he has no ownership rights on his own body, which, it is argued, belongs not to him but to God. A man can do whatever he wishes with his property provided no harm is caused thereby to others. But he has as few property rights over his own body as he has over the bodies of others. This chapter seeks to demonstrate that the individual does, on the contrary, enjoy considerable autonomy so far as his body is concerned.

We begin with the statement in the Mishnah (*Bava Kama* 8:9), elaborated on in the Gemara (*Bava Kama* 91b), that Rabbi Akiba ruled, 'If a man wounds himself, even though he has no right so to do, he is not culpable; but if others have wounded him they are culpable.' To this the Mishnah adds, 'If a man cut down his own plants, though he has no right so to do, he is not culpable; but if others cut them down they are culpable.' The Mishnah uses exactly the same expression – 'though he has no right so to do' – for both a man wounding himself and a man who cuts down shoots, seeming to imply that the same reasoning is behind the two cases and that no distinction is made in this matter between a man's body and his property.

The Gemara, elaborating on the Mishnah, states that the opinion of the Mishnah is not a unanimous one, and a *Baraita* is quoted in which the opposite opinion is stated, that a man commits no wrong if he inflicts an injury on his own body. Who is the Tanna of the Mishnah? the Gemara asks, i.e. where else do we find a Tannaitic statement to the effect that it is wrong to inflict an injury on oneself? The Gemara first suggests that the Tanna is R Eleazar, who derives from a Scriptural verse that suicide is strictly forbidden. But, the Gemara objects, it by no means follows that because a man is forbidden to take his own life he is not allowed to inflict an injury on his own body. In the one case he destroys a human life, albeit his own, whereas in the other there is no destruction of life. Another Tanna is then quoted who holds that to destroy one's clothes is to offend against the prohibition against wanton destruction of objects. This is known as *bal tashḥit*,' 'do not destroy', and is based on the verse prohibiting the destruction of fruit-bearing trees (Deuteronomy 20:19). If a man, according to this Tanna, must not even destroy his clothes it must surely follow that he is not allowed to engage in such destructive practices as self-injury. No, the Gemara continues, it does not follow that because clothes may not be destroyed self-injury is forbidden since where clothes are destroyed the destruction is total whereas a body that has suffered an injury can be healed, i.e. and, possibly, the prohibition of *bal tashḥit* applies only where the loss is irreparable. Finally, the Gemara concludes, the Tanna with whose view the Mishnah concurs is R. Eleazar Hakkapar, who declares that it is sinful to fast because it is a denial of God's gifts and by the same token self-injury is forbidden.[2] The reason why the Mishnah states, in the second clause, that it is forbidden to destroy the shoots is obviously because of *bal tashḥit* and, the Gemara states, the prohibition of self-injury is either for the same reason or because it is, like fasting, a rejection of God's gifts.

From all this it emerges that the opinion in the Mishnah, 'a man has no right to wound himself', is not unanimous. Moreover, the reason, according to the final analysis in the Gemara, is either because of 'waste' or because he rejects God's gift of a healthy body just as the one who fasts rejects God's gifts. There is nothing in the whole discussion to warrant the view that a man has no ownership rights over his body. On the contrary, the whole *sugya* in the Gemara appears to suggest the opposite, that a man does own his body, since the reason of 'waste' obviously applies to property as well, which he does own. At this stage of the discussion, at any rate, a man owns his body as much as he owns his property. And even when the Gemara introduces the idea of 'denial' this is surely not an about turn. That, *according to one opinion*, a man must not deny himself surely does not mean that he does not own his body. If anything, the opposite is suggested even here. God has *given* him his body, which he must care for in gratitude for the divine gift.

To turn now to Maimonides (*Yad Ḥovel u-Mazzik* 5:1). This great Codifier compares the prohibition of a man wounding himself to the prohibition of wounding his fellow. The prohibition of wounding another cannot be because a man does not 'own' the body of his fellow. Obviously, he does not. According to Maimonides, it all falls under the heading of 'wounding an Israelite',[3] though it is probable that Maimonides states the rule that self-injury is forbidden simply in juxtaposition to wounding another without necessarily holding that the reason is the same in both instances. But, even if this is so, there is not the slightest suggestion that the reason for the prohibition of self-injury is because a man does not own his body. The *Shulḥan 'Arukh* (*Ḥoshen Mishpat* 620:39) records the prohibition of wounding oneself separately from that of wounding one's fellow.

Despite what seems to be perfectly clear from the sources, as above, S. J. Sevin[4] purports to find what he calls 'a marvellous point' (*nekudah niflaah*) in the *Shulḥan 'Arukh* of R Shneor Zalman of Liady,[5] according to which the reason for the ruling in the Mishnah is that a man's body is not his but God's. In R Shneor Zalman's formulation the rule reads: 'It is forbidden for a man to smite his fellow even if the latter gives him permission so to do. For a man has no right at all [*eyn le-adam reshut kelel*] over his body that he should be allowed to smite it.' Sevin understands R Shneor Zalman to be saying that the reason why self-mutilation is forbidden is because a man's body does not belong to him, that he should be allowed to inflict an injury on it, but to God. It is God's property, with which he is not allowed to interfere. R Shneor Zalman does not, in fact, quite say this. He does not say, 'A man has no rights in his body and *therefore* he cannot give another permission to smite it.' He simply says 'he has no right to smite his body', which may be no more than a restatement of the rule of the Mishnah as amplified in the Gemara. Sevin, however, understands him to be saying, in Sevin's words, 'The body is not his and he is not the owner of his body' (*eyn ha-guf she-lo ve-eyn hu ha-be'alim al gufo*), a very far-reaching concept which, as we have noted, finds no support in any of the earlier sources.

Sevin does try to find support for the view which he reads into R Shneor Zalman's formulation in another ruling of Maimonides (*Yad Rotzeaḥ* 1:4). Here Maimonides rules that if a murderer wishes to buy himself out of the death penalty (by paying compensation to the heirs of his victim) he is not allowed to do this even if the Avenger of the Blood (Numbers chapter 35) is willing for the murderer to be exonerated 'for the person (*nefesh*) of the victim does not belong to the Avenger of the Blood but to the Holy One, blessed be He'.

According to Sevin, Maimonides adds 'but to the Holy One, blessed be He' in order to state that a man's body is not his but God's. But Maimonides is dealing with a case of murder. The body of the victim is in no way the issue since it is dead and gone. It is the 'person', the *nefesh*, the *life taken*, that is at issue. Maimonides is saying that the Avenger of the Blood has no standing in the matter when the question arises of freeing the murderer from his punishment. It is God's business, so to speak, to avenge the life that He gave and the murderer took away, even though He has appointed, in the Torah, the Avenger of the Blood to see to it that the vengeance is carried out. This has nothing whatever to do with the question of whether a living man's body belongs to him or to God.

Sevin finds further support for his view in a comment of R David Ibn Abi Zimra, the *Radbaz*, in his Commentary to Maimonides (*Yad, Sanhedrin* 18:6). Here Maimonides states that it is a 'divine decree' (*gezerat ha-katuv*) that, while when a man admits that he owes someone a sum of money he is believed, yet if he confesses that he is a murderer or that he has committed an offence for which he is liable to a flogging (*malkut*) he is not believed. *Radbaz* observes that it is, indeed, a 'divine decree' yet some 'slight reason' can be given to explain the distinction between an admission in a monetary case and a confession of guilt deserving of capital or corporal punishment. *Radbaz* quotes the verse, 'Behold, all souls are Mine' (Jeremiah 18:4). All souls belong to God. Hence a man cannot be convicted in a capital charge on his own testimony for that would be equivalent to him giving away that which belongs not to him but to God, his life. As for *malkut*, this is equivalent to a man giving up part of his life, since '*malkut* is half a death'.[6]

First, it should be noted that *Radbaz* is doing the exercise of discovering 'reasons for the *mitzvot* (*ta'amey ha-mitzvot*) and it is generally accepted, even by its practitioners, that the 'reasons' they discover are on the Aggadic not the Halakhic level. Secondly, *Radbaz* admits that what he suggests is only in the nature of a 'slight reason' and that ultimately one must fall back on the idea of a 'divine decree'. But, apart from all this, *Radbaz* does not say that a man's *body* is not his but God's. Rather he says that a man's *life* is not his to dispose of if he sees fit to commit suicide by testifying that he has committed a murder which, even if he did commit it, brings capital punishment in its wake only where there are witnesses to the crime. If this were not so, but because a man does not 'own' his body, what reason did *Radbaz* have for introducing the notion of *malkut* as half a death?[7] Even if *malkut* were not 'half a death', it would still be wrong, on Sevin's understanding of the matter, to injure that which does not belong to him but to God.

In short, Sevin and other recent authors who follow the same line have not succeeded in reading into the classical sources the idea that a man's body is not his own but belongs to God.[8]

If we are to apply Halakhic categories to our question, it can be asked, if the Sevin view is correct, how can a man impose restrictions on his body by a vow and thus contradict the rule that a man cannot impose a prohibition on that which does not belong to him (*eyn adam oser davar she-eyno she-lo*)?[9] And, for that matter, how can a man sell himself as a Hebrew slave[10] since a man cannot sell something that does not belong to him?

Naturally, from the theological point of view everything belongs to God, but that would apply to property as well. Only confusion results if this theological idea is applied to the human body alone.[11] And even from the theological view there is a sense in which it is true that God has given the earth to the children of man.

CHAPTER 9

Worship with the body

In Judaism, as in other religions, the tensions, even the dichotomy, between body and soul are certainly not unknown yet it is axiomatic in every version of a faith correctly described as the religion of *doing* God's will that the body is to be brought into play at every stage of the religious life. The *mitzvot*, the precepts of the Torah, to be sure, are not limited to the performance of bodily actions. Some of the *mitzvot* such as the love of God and the neighbour have to do with emotional, psychological states. But the majority of the *mitzvot* are in the nature of commands to carry out this or that physical act and to refrain from this or that physical act. The hugely influential, Sufi-inspired, mediaeval classic, *Duties of the Heart*, by Bahya Ibn Pakudah (twelfth century)[1] appeals for greater inwardness in the religious life. In Bahya's terminology adopted from the Sufis, the *mitzvot* are divided into 'duties of the heart' and 'duties of the limbs' and it is the former that need to be emphasized. All very true, and yet even Bahya, the most determined advocate of inwardness, cannot, and does not, ignore the 'duties of the limbs'. We know very little about Bahya's life but we do know that he was a strictly observant Jew and a *dayan* (a judge) to boot.

A typical Talmudic saying[2] has it that there are 248 positive precepts of the Torah corresponding to the 248 'limbs' (i.e. parts) of the human body and there are 365 negative precepts corresponding to the 365 days in the solar years. In a later Midrashic comment[3] this is amplified: 'The 248 positive precepts correspond to the 248 limbs of the body, each saying: "I beg of you perform this *mitzvah* with me." And the 365 negative precepts correspond to the 365 days of the solar year, each saying: "I beg of you do not commit on me this sin."'

In the Jewish mystical tradition the human being is written large, as it were, in the universe; the human body having cosmic significance. From the work *Shi'ur Komah*,[4] which describes in rich and bewildering detail the dimensions of the mystical body of God, through the Zohar and the Kabbalah in general, the divine 'body' is the source on high of the physical body on earth, with the implication that when the individual human body is engaged in the performance of good deeds beneficent influences are sent heavenwards to promote the flow of the divine grace throughout creation and when evil deeds are carried out baneful influences are sent on high to arrest the flow of the divine grace. The Ten *Sefirot*, the powers or potencies in the Godhead, are frequently described in terms of a body. For instance, the passage in *Tikkuney Zohar* known as 'Elijah's Praise'[5] reads:

Elijah began to praise God, saying: Lord of the Universe! Thou art One but art not numbered. Thou art higher than the highest. Thou art the mystery above all mysteries. No thought can grasp Thee at all. It is Thou who produced the Ten Perfections that we call the Ten *Sefirot*. With them Thou guidest the secret worlds that have not been revealed and in them Thou dost conceal Thyself from human beings. But it is Thou who bindest them together and unitest them. Since Thou art in them, whoever separates any of the ten from the others it is as if he had made a division in Thee... This is the order that they follow: *Ḥesed* [Lovingkindness] is the right arm; *Gevurah* [Power] is the left arm; *Tiferet* [Beauty] the torso; *Netzaḥ* [Victory] and *Hod* [Splendour] the two legs; *Yesod* [Foundation] the extremity of the body, the holy sign of the covenant; *Malkhut* [Sovereignty] the mouth, called the Oral Law. The brain is *Ḥokhmah* [Wisdom], the inner thoughts. *Binah* [Understanding] is in the heart and of this we say: 'the heart understands.' With regard to these two, Scripture says: 'The secret things belong unto the Lord our God' (Deuteronomy 29:28). The elevated *Keter* [Crown] is the Crown of Sovereignty, and of it Scripture says: 'Declaring the end from the beginning' (Isaiah 46:10). It is the skull upon which the *tefillin* are placed. From within it is *yod*, *hey*, *vav*, *hey*, which is the path of emanation. It provides the water for the tree, its arms and its branches, just as a tree grows when it is watered. Lord of the Universe! Thou art the Cause of causes, the Ground of grounds, Who waterest the tree by means of a spring and this spring is as the soul to the body, by means of which the body survives. In Thee there is no likeness or image of anything within or without.

Elsewhere in the *Tikkuney Zohar*[6] it is stated that each limb of 'The King' is a *mitzvah*; i.e. the precepts form, as it were, the mystical divine corpus.[7] In the Zohar proper[8] it is spelled out in detail that the human body is a microcosm so that the skin, flesh, bones and sinews all have their symbolic meaning in the mystery of the

Supernal wisdom. The bones and sinews correspond to the divine Chariot and the Heavenly hosts. The flesh is a covering to these chariots and hosts and is symbolically connected with the demonic forces. The skin corresponds to the firmament covering all things. But all these are merely garments to the inner human being and so it is on high. This is said to be the meaning of 'And God created man in His own image; in the image of God created He him' (Genesis 1:27).

Despite the strong opposition to the Kabbalah at first, eventually ideas such as these became acceptable so that when studying how the individual body functions in Jewish worship it is no distortion to refer to practices and rituals based on the Kabbalah as well as those based on the more conventional sources of the Bible, the Talmud and the Codes. In this chapter I want to examine the subject under five headings: (1) The use of the body in prayer; (2) Dress and deportment of the body; (3) Eating and drinking as acts of worship; (4) Sex; (5) Some other aspects.

The use of the body in prayer

In all the sources it is emphasized that the body be cleansed before prayer by evacuation of the bowels and the passing of water. The Kabbalists add the further motif that the waste products of the body represent the demonic forces and these have to be eliminated if they are not to hinder the ascent of the prayers. The Talmud[9] states that if a man needs to ease himself but recites his prayers without doing so, his prayer is an abomination. The text quoted in support is, 'Prepare to meet thy God, O Israel' (Amos 4:12), understood to mean: Prepare your body by cleansing it of its waste before you meet your God in prayer. Similarly, the verse, 'Guard thy foot when thou goest to the house of God' (Ecclesiastes 4:17) is made to read, 'Guard thy orifices at the time of standing in prayer.' The standard Code of Jewish practice, the *Shulḥan 'Arukh*, compiled by Joseph Karo with glosses by Moses Isserles in the sixteenth century, codifies all this[10] in the section on the regulations for prayer as well as devoting a special section to the need for modest behaviour in the privy. This latter is placed near the beginning of the Code as one of the first obligations to be carried out when rising from sleep.[11] A typical Kabbalistic understanding is provided by the Hasidic master, Mordecai of Chernobil (d. 1837), who writes:[12]

When a man rises in the morning he should get up energetically to serve his Creator, blessed be He, to be a faithful servant to Him. As the *Shulḥan 'Arukh* rules, he should first evacuate his bowels in order to push away the waste so as to give the wicked one [i.e. Satan] his portion so that he should not be envious and seek to enjoy the holy. It is also in order to avoid vapours ascending from the dung to the mind since if that happens the mind can become contaminated with strange thoughts of unbelief and fornication and thus invalidate the sacrifice of the brain, the temple of the Lord.

The Talmud[13] followed by the *Shulḥan 'Arukh*[14] gives the benediction to be recited after attending to bodily functions:

Blessed is He who has formed man in wisdom and created in him many cavities. It is fully known before the throne of Thy glory that if one of them should be improperly opened or one of them closed it would be impossible for a man to stand before Thee, Blessed art Thou Who healest all flesh and doeth wonderfully.

The ritual washing of the hands, water being poured from a jug or bowl three times on each hand, takes place immediately on rising.[15] Two reasons have been advanced for this ritual. The first is that during sleep the hands may have touched parts of the body that are usually covered and it is improper to worship God without washing away the resulting contamination. The other reason is that, at the beginning of the day, a human being is as one newly created to serve his Maker. Like the practice of the priests in the Temple, who bathed their hands and feet in the laver before beginning their service, each human being must make similar preparations. The Kabbalists supply a further reason. A spirit of impurity descends on the sleeping body. This leaves the whole body except for the hands when one awakes and must be banished from the hands, too, by the ritual bathing. The commentator to the *Shulḥan 'Arukh*, Abraham Gombiner (d. 1683), quotes[16] the Talmudic passage[17] that each day a man should wash his face, hands and feet for the glory of God in whose image he is created.[18] The washing of the feet was observed, however, only by Jews residing in Muslim lands! Relevant to the idea of bathing for the glory of God is the story told in the Midrash[19] of Hillel who, on his way to the bathhouse, said to his disciples that he was on the way to perform a religious duty. 'Is it a religious duty to bathe?', they asked. 'Yes', replied Hillel. 'If the statues of kings erected in theatres and circuses are regularly scoured and washed by the one appointed to look after them, how much more I, who have been created in God's image and likeness.'

According to the Rabbinic interpretation of the Song of Songs as a dialogue between God and the Jewish people, the male hero of the Song is God. On the basis of this the later Kabbalists[20] advise that when the face and hands are washed a number of verses from the Song of Songs should be in the mind. Thus when washing the hands one should have in mind the verse, 'His hands are as rolls of gold set with beryl' (Song of Songs 5:14); when washing the forehead the verse, 'His head is as the most fine gold' (5:11); the eyes, 'His eyes are like doves' (5:12); the cheeks, 'His cheeks are as a bed of spices, as banks of sweet herbs' (5:13); the lips, 'His lips are as lilies, dropping with flowing myrrh' (5:13); the mouth, 'His body is as polished ivory, overlaid with sapphires (5:14). When the face is dried with the hand towel after it has been washed, the verse from the prophetic vision of God and the Chariot is recited: 'As for the likeness of their faces, they had the face of a man; and they four had the face of a lion on the right side' (Ezekiel 1:10).

The Talmud[21] rules that it is not necessary to have total immersion in a spring or ritual bath (*mikveh*) before prayer but the Hasidim attached great significance to this act of purification before the early morning prayer. In Hasidic teaching, when the naked body is immersed in the natural water of the *mikveh* then, just as the body is totally covered by the pure water, the *ḥasid* attains to the state known as 'annihilation of self', that is, loss of selfhood in God.[22]

In another application of the verse, 'Prepare to meet thy God, O Israel' (Amos 4:12) the Talmud[23] states that it is proper to wear a girdle around the loins when praying. The French mediaeval glossarists, the Tosafists, in their commentary to the Talmudic passage in which this is said, remark that the reason for it is to have a division between the upper and lower part of the body; in the language of the tradition, that the heart 'should not see' the genitals, from which they draw the conclusion that in mediaeval France, where the trousers were kept up by a belt, there was no need to wear a special girdle for prayer. Nevertheless, the *Shulḥan 'Arukh*[24] rules, on the basis of the Talmudic quote from Amos, that even if a belt is worn it is still necessary to don the special girdle for prayer, and all Hasidic Jews wear for prayer a special girdle of twined silk.

For the morning prayers the body is wrapped around with the *tallit* ('prayer shawl'). The *Shulḥan 'Arukh* states[25] that ideally the *tallit* should cover most of the body. Many pious Jews wear the *tallit* over the head so that both head and most of the body are enclosed in a world of their own, so to speak, with no distractions from without and alone with God.

The *tefillin* ('phylacteries') are also worn for the morning prayer but not for the afternoon and evening prayers. The hand *tefillin* is placed on the upper left arm, turned towards the heart, and the straps attached to it are wound seven times around the arm. Then the head *tefillin* is placed on the hair in the middle of the head directly above the nose and forehead.[26] The prayer books have a meditation for putting on the *tallit* and another one for the *tefillin*. The meditation before putting on the *tallit* reads:[27]

I am here enwrapping myself in this fringed robe, in fulfilment of the command of my Creator, as it is written in the Law: 'They shall make them a fringe upon the corners of their garments throughout their generations.' And even as I cover myself with the *tallit* in this world, so may my soul deserve to be clothed with a beauteous spiritual robe in the world to come, in the garden of Eden. Amen.

The meditation before putting on the *tefillin*[28] reads:

I am here intent upon the act of putting on the *tefillin* in fulfilment of the command of my Creator... He has commanded us to lay the *tefillin* upon the hand as a memorial of the outstretched arm; opposite the heart, to indicate the duty of subjecting the longings and designs of our heart to His service, blessed be He; and upon the head over against the brain, thereby teaching that the mind, whose seat is in the brain, together with all senses and faculties, is to be subjected to His service, Blessed be He. Amen.

The practice of swaying the body while studying the Torah is attested to in the Zohar[29] and in the *Kuzari*[30] of R Judah Halevi (eleventh–twelfth century). The Zohar explains the practice on the grounds that when a tiny candle flame is confronted with a gigantic fire the flame moves towards the fire. The soul's movement towards the spiritual light of the Torah causes the body to sway automatically. Halevi, on the other hand, offers a rationalistic explanation. In ancient times, he argues, copies of the sacred books were few so that a number of students had to sit round the same copy, with the result that, as they read, they were obliged to incline the body the better to see the text. It would seem, then, that in the thirteenth century, the date of the Zohar, swaying took place only while studying the Torah, but the practice was soon extended to prayer. In his gloss to the *Shulḥan 'Arukh*, Isserles[31] quotes earlier authorities who advocate swaying in prayer on the basis of the verse, 'All my bones shall say, Lord, who is like unto Thee?' (Psalm

35:10). Gombiner in his note to this passage quotes authorities who advocate swaying in prayer and others who frown on it as lacking in decorum and he concludes:[32] 'It is proper to hold to either of these opinions provided it assists concentration.' Hasidim, in particular, prefer violent swaying to and fro in their prayers. To the scandal of the traditionalist Rabbis in the eighteenth century, some of the Hasidim would go so far as to turn somersaults during their prayers as an exercise in overcoming the grasping ego.[33]

The *Shulḥan 'Arukh*[34] refers to the custom of covering the eyes with the right hand while reciting the first verse of the Shema: 'Hear, O Israel! The Lord our God, the Lord is One' (Deuteronomy 6:4). As the *Shulḥan 'Arukh* puts it, 'It is customary to place the hand over the face while reciting the first verse as an aid to concentration'; i.e. in order to avoid distraction, the eyes are covered and the gaze directed inwards.

The practice of beating the breast when reciting the confession of sins, especially on the Day of Atonement, is referred to in the Midrash:[35] 'R Mano said, "And the living will lay it to his heart" (Ecclesiastes 7:2): these are the righteous who set their death against their heart; and why do they beat upon their heart? As though to say, "All is thee".' The hand beating the breast is symbolic of the deed which results from the evil designs of the heart.[36]

In the section of the prayers known as the *Kedushah* ('Sanctification') the song of the Seraphim is repeated: 'And one called to the other, "Holy, holy, holy! The Lord of Hosts! His presence fills the earth"' (Isaiah 6:3). Of the angels bearing the Chariot in Ezekiel's vision (Ezekiel 1:7) the verse says, 'the legs of each were [fused into] a simple rigid leg'. On the basis of these two verses the *Shulḥan 'Arukh*[37] states, 'It is good to place the feet together when the *Kedusha* is recited.' Isserles adds, 'The eyes should be raised on high when the *Kedushah* is recited and the body should also be raised from the ground', i.e. reaching upwards towards the Heavenly Throne. Similarly, with regard to posture during the statutory prayer, the *'Amidah*, the *Shulḥan 'Arukh*[38] writes, 'He should place his feet together as if they were a single foot in order to resemble the angels of whom it is said, "the legs of each were a single leg", that is to say, they appeared to be a single leg.' The custom is to take three paces forwards before beginning the *'Amidah* and three paces backwards at the end in order to draw nearer to the King at the beginning and bow out of His presence at the end.[39]

Gesture in prayer goes back to Bible times. There are references in the Bible to bending the knee in prayer (I Kings 8:54; Isaiah 45:23); prostration on the face (Exodus 34:8; Psalms 29:2); the spreading of the hands heavenwards (I Kings 8:23; Isaiah 1:15; and, possibly, the placing of the head between the knees (I Kings 18:42). The standard practice of bowing head and body at the beginning and end of the *'Amidah* is mentioned in the Talmud.[40] On bowing the head and body at the words, 'Blessed art Thou, O Lord', the Talmud[41] states that one should bow at the word 'Blessed' but should return to the upright position before reciting 'O Lord'; this on the basis of the verse, 'The Lord raiseth up them that are bowed down' (Psalm 146:8). Of R Sheshet it is said that he used to bend like a reed (i.e. with one simple movement) but used to raise himself slowly 'like a serpent'. In yet another Talmudic passage[42] it is said that when bowing at the appropriate places one should bow low until all the vertebrae in the spinal column are loosened. All these statements have been adopted as the norm in Jewish prayer.

The practice of raising the hands in prayer is not widely followed but is advocated in the Zohar, the ten fingers representing the Ten *Sefirot*.[43] The practice is strongly advocated, too, by the Kabbalist Alexander Süsskind of Grodno (d. 1793) in his compendium of worship, *Yesod ve-Shoresh ha-'Avodah*.[44] He writes:

> Friends and brethren! How can a man fail to be on fire to perform this tremendous act [of raising the hands on high] of worship! It is so easy to carry out yet there is incomparable and limitless worth in the act. For all the holy worlds on high become united and sanctified as a result of this act of worship and all the denizens of the 'Other Side' are subdued and laid low.

It is the practice of Orthodox, Conservative and many Reform Jews to have the head covered for prayer. Although this does not appear to have been mandatory at first it is now the well-nigh universal practice. To cover the head, in the East, is a sign of reverence while bare-headedness denotes lack of respect.[45]

In the Jewish tradition the words of the prayers have to be voiced; merely to dwell on the words in the mind is insufficient. There are also traditional melodies to suit the mood and context of various prayers. Here, too, while inwardness is strongly advocated, the physical act – here the mouthing of the words – is essential. Some have understood this on the basis of the old psychological principle, there is no impression without expression. The sacred dance (David dancing before the Lord in II Samuel 6:14–16 is the classical example) is, nowadays, limited mainly to Hasidic groups, except on the festival of *Simḥat Torah* ('Rejoicing in the Law'), when the congregation take the Scrolls of the Torah in a procession around the synagogue and dance with the Scrolls.

In Bible times, a priest with bodily blemishes was disqualified from serving in the Temple.

> No man of your offspring throughout the ages who has a defect shall be qualified; no man who is blind, or lame, or has a limb too short or too long; no man who has a broken leg or a broken arm; or who is a hunchback, or a dwarf, or who has a growth in his eye, or who has a boil-scar, or scurvy, or crushed testes. No men among the offspring of Aaron the priest who has a defect shall be qualified to offer the Lord's offerings by fire; having a defect, he shall not be qualified to offer the food of his God
>
> (Leviticus 21:17–21).

Do bodily defects disqualify a person from serving as a prayer leader (cantor) in the synagogue? This question was discussed in a Responsum of Meir b. Baruch of Rottenburg (d. 1293).[46] Meir argues that the disqualification applied only to priests serving in the Temple. On the contrary, says Baruch, a cripple is especially suited to lead the prayers in the synagogue since, unlike a human king who throws away broken vessels, God prefers His broken vessels, as the Psalmist says, 'A broken and a contrite heart, O God, Thou wilt not despise' (Psalm 51:19). Abraham Gombiner,[47] however, refers to the Zohar where it is implied that a person with physical defects should not lead the congregation in prayer.

Dress and deportment of the body

The *Shulḥan 'Arukh* has a whole section on dress and deportment of the body,[48] based mainly on the Talmud. Among the regulations recorded here are the following. Care should be taken, when sleeping naked, to put on the shirt and underclothes, on waking, under the bed covers since even though no other human being may see God sees. The shirt should not be worn inside out. Since right is symbolic of the good and the true, the right shoe should be put on before the left shoe and when taking off the shoes the left should be removed first. A person should not walk about barefoot and should wear clothes that cover the whole body adequately. It is wrong to walk with a stiff, upright posture, out of respect for the glory of God that fills the universe.

The verse, 'You shall not round off the side-growth on your head, or destroy the side-growth of your beard' (Leviticus 19:27), is interpreted in the Rabbinic tradition to mean that a man must have a small side-growth of hair near the ears but it is forbidden to remove other facial hair only with a razor. Thus there is nothing wrong for a Jewish male to be clean-shaven provided that the hair is removed with other than a razor, understood as a single blade. (This is why many observant Jews shave with an electric razor.) However, until modern times the majority of observant Jews did sport a beard. The Talmud refers to the beard as 'the adornment of the face'. The majority of Hasidic Jews not only wear beards (some never touch the beard to trim it, leaving it to grow long) and not only have 'corners of the head' (*peot*) of the minimum length but cultivate lengthy *peot*, often in 'corkscrew' shape. Behind this is the Kabbalistic view that the beard and *peot* represent the streams of unimpeded mercy from the highest of the *Sefirot* to the lower and from there down through all worlds. A young scholar has recently written a large volume with the title *The Adornment of the Face – The Beard*, in which he seeks to prove from the sources that observant Jews should wear beards.[49]

The *Shulḥan 'Arukh*[50] states that in honour of the Sabbath the whole body should be bathed in hot water on the eve of the Sabbath and if the hair is too long it should be cut. The nails should be cut on the eve of the Sabbath. Isserles[51] quotes earlier authorities to the effect that the nails should not be cut in the order of the fingers but on the right hand the order should be: the second finger, the fourth, the thumb, the third and the little finger. On the left hand the order should be: the fourth finger, the second, the little finger, the third and the thumb, though the reason for this strange order is not stated. Gombiner[52] observes that the famous Kabbalist, Isaac Luria, ridiculed this practice as sheer superstition. Nevertheless Gombiner advises that the practice be followed in the first instance.

Men are not permitted to wear women's garments and women to wear men's (Deuteronomy 22:3). Another law observed by traditional Jews is that contained in the verse, 'You shall not wear a garment in which wool and linen are combined' (Deuteronomy 22:11). This latter was one of the reasons why the early Hasidim in the eighteenth century wore only coats of silk, i.e. in order to avoid the slightest possibility of wearing a garment of wool and linen combined. Because of their fondness for silk the Hasidim were dubbed 'Chinamen' by some of their opponents. Nowadays, the majority of Hasidim wear silken coats only in honour of the Sabbath and Festivals. Also on the Sabbath many Hasidim wear the *streimel*, the sable hat originally the headgear worn by the Polish aristocracy from whom the Hasidim adopted it. But later on various mystical ideas were read into the wearing of the *streimel*, e.g. that it has 13 sable or mink tails corresponding to the thirteen qualities of the divine mercy. Jews influenced by the Kabbalah always button their jackets and coats right on left since in the Sefirotic scheme the *Sefirot* on the right side represent mercy, those on the left judgement.[53]

Eating and drinking as acts of worship

Although ascetic tendencies are not absent from Rabbinic Judaism, the general or prevailing view is that God gives man the pleasures of the world to enjoy provided that man acknowledges his indebtedness to his Creator by reciting a benediction for the food and drink he enjoys. In Hasidism the idea developed that since, as the Kabbalists say, there are 'holy sparks' in all created things and these have to be rescued for the holy from the forces of evil by which they are imprisoned, it is essential to eat and drink with the express intention of serving God by rescuing the 'sparks' and elevating the food and drink. Thus every meal becomes a sacred meal.

The meals partaken of on the Sabbath and Festivals are especially sacred meals, particularly, the *Seder*, the festive meal on the first night of Passover, at which are eaten the unleavened bread and the bitter herbs as a reminder of the Exodus and on which night four cups of wine are imbibed while singing God's praises for His deliverances. During Tabernacles meals are partaken of in the *sukkah*, the tent-like structure that serves as a reminder of the tents in which the Israelites dwelt during their forty years' journey through the wilderness.[54]

In Hasidism in particular the sacred meal has a special place. On the Sabbath and the Festivals the Hasidim sit at the table of the Zaddik, the Hasidic saint, to listen to his exposition of 'Torah', that is, his original exposition of Hasidic doctrines and themes. At these meals, the Zaddik first takes a small quantity of food from each dish set before him, the remainder being distributed among his followers, in the belief that food the Zaddik has first tasted contains both spiritual and physical blessing.

Sex

The Biblical references to 'be fruitful and multiply' (Genesis 1:28; 9:1) are understood in the Rabbinic tradition as an injunction to marry and have children. For this reason celibacy as a religious ideal never gained much of a foothold in normative Judaism. The second-century sage, Ben Azzai, as we have noted earlier, is reported to have said in defence of his refusal to marry[55] that his soul was too much in love with the Torah for him to take an earthly wife. The *Shulḥan 'Arukh*[56] accepts celibacy as an alternative life-style: 'One whose soul is in love with the Torah like Ben Azzai and who cleaves to it all his days and never marries commits no sin provided his sexual instincts do not get the better of him.' Nevertheless, very few indeed followed the celibate way. But Judaism has always been very strict in forbidding all extra-marital sexual activity.[57] Masturbation is denounced both in the Talmudic literature and in the Kabbalah. In the latter, for a male to keep remote from sexual thoughts that might lead to loss of semen is called 'keeping the sign of the covenant', i.e. preserving in complete purity the organ upon which circumcision is made, circumcision being the 'covenant with Abraham' (Genesis 17:9–14). All this is, of course, in the books. To what extent observant Jews actually follow these rules is hard to know.

In the Kabbalah, the sex act mirrors the 'sacred marriage' on high, the union of the *Sefirot Tiferet* and *Malkhut*, representing respectively the male and female principles in the Godhead, and is, consequently, of great spiritual significance. It is a religious act to be engaged in in a spirit of sanctification and purity. In some Kabbalistic writings[58] the details of the act, from kissing, embracing through to coitus itself, are described so as to correspond to the various combinations among the Sefirot. Hayyim Vital, pupil of Isaac Luria, in his rules for regulating the life of the Kabbalist, writes:[59] 'He should sanctify himself at the time of intercourse so that he derives no pleasure from the act', i.e. but should carry it out solely as a re-enactment of the supernal mysteries.

The early Kabbalist and renowned Talmudist, Nahmanides (1195–1270), compiled a special treatise on the performance of the sex act with the revealing title, 'Iggeret ha-Kodesh', 'The Holy Letter',[60] at the beginning of which he states that the act is holy if performed in the right spirit, and he takes strong issue with Maimonides' acceptance[61] of the Aristotelian dictum that the sense of touch is shameful. Aristotle, Nahmanides suggests, held that matter is eternal, which is why he can describe the act as shameful, since God and matter are separated from eternity, whereas the Jewish view sees God as the Creator of matter and the human body. That which God has created cannot be 'shameful'.

Some further aspects

A compendium, *Meah Berakhot*, 'One Hundred Benedictions', listing all the benedictions to be recited by the pious Jew, was published in Amsterdam in the year 1687. On the frontispiece of this little book there is an artist's impression of how each of the five senses is brought into play and the special benediction over each of these. For sight, the picture is of Jews reciting the blessing over the new moon; they gaze up at the moon as they recite the benediction. For hearing, the picture is of the ram's horn sounded on the festival of Rosh ha-Shanah. For taste, the illustration is of three persons saying grace over food they have eaten; three because then a special introduction is recited. For the sense of touch, the picture is of a circumcision. Finally, for the sense of smell, there is the *Havdalah* ceremony at the termination of the Sabbath, when sweet spices are smelled in order to restore the soul and at the departure of the Sabbath.

During the *Havdalah* ceremony a plaited candle is lit and God thanked for the gift of light. It is customary to look at the finger nails by the light of the candle and to spread out the fingers of the hand. The origin of this is obscure but it has been interpreted to denote that the hands, idle on the Sabbath in obedience to the command to abstain from work, can now be opened for weekday activities.

There is a particularly interesting use of hands in worship. This is when the priestly blessing (Numbers 6:12–27) is recited, the *tallit* covering the head and with outstretched hands.[62] The fingers of the hands of the priests are arranged so as to form five cavities or 'windows'. This is based on the verse in the Song of Songs (2:9) 'gazing through the windows', God sending His blessings, so to speak, through the openings between the fingers of the priests.

Other examples of worship with the body are: rising before the aged and those learned in the Torah;[63] running to the synagogue and to places where the Torah is studied;[64] elevating the open Scroll of the Torah and showing the sacred text to the congregation on the days when the Torah is read from the Scroll; kissing sacred objects such as the prayer book and the *tefillin*; and taking the Scrolls in solemn procession around the synagogue. When this is done, the custom is for the congregants to bow to the Scroll, though some authorities frown on this as an implied worship of the Torah. Only God is to be the Object of worship.

To keep the body healthy and care for it is a religious duty. Maimonides[65] describes the ideal of *mens sana in corpore sano* in its Jewish form as follows:

> Since for the body to be healthy and whole belongs to God's way – for it is impossible to understand or to know anything about the knowledge of God when one is sick – it is necessary to keep away from anything that is destructive of the body and one is obliged to do that which brings healing to the body.

Maimonides, as a physician himself, proceeds to advise how good health is to be promoted. In the Rabbinic tradition generally, the health of the body comes first so that if a person is ordered by his doctor to eat on the Day of Atonement, for instance, otherwise his life may be endangered, he is obliged to eat as a religious duty.

Traditional Jews are opposed to cremation, chiefly on the ground that the body, which served as the vehicle of the soul and with which the precepts were carried out, should not be destroyed but allowed to turn to dust of its own accord through burial in the soil. Similarly, there is much opposition to the performance of autopsies unless it be for the purpose of saving life. The Kabbalah has come to have a marked influence on burial rites. Various Kabbalistic manuals describe how each limb of the corpse is to be washed while Biblical references to that limb are recited.[66] The Kabbalistic understanding of the image of God idea is applied here. For instance, when the head of the corpse is washed the verse is recited, 'His head is finest gold' (Song of Songs 5:11); when the cheeks are washed, the verse is recited, 'His cheeks are like beds of spices' (Song of Songs 5:13).

Traditionally, the doctrine of the resurrection of the dead refers to bodily resurrection. Maimonides and Nahmanides are divided on this issue, as they are divided on the question of sex. According to Maimonides it is the soul alone that is immortal. Maimonides does believe in a physical resurrection but holds that eventually the revived dead will return to dust, the soul alone basking in the radiance of the Shekhinah in Paradise for all eternity. Nahmanides, on the other hand, believes that the resurrected dead will live on for ever in the body, albeit in a vastly more refined body.[67]

This chapter may fittingly conclude with a note on how the mediaeval Jewish authors[68] used the verse, 'From my flesh I behold God' (Job 19:26). These interpreted the verse to mean that man can know God through contemplating the workings of his own mind and body. Among the Kabbalists, especially the human body, not only the soul, mirrors forth the divine: 'And from my *flesh* I behold God.'

CHAPTER 10

God and personal freedom

In the previous chapters we considered how far individuality of soul and of body extends in relation to God. In this chapter will be considered how individual free-will operates in that relationship.

If God knows beforehand how man will conduct himself in the future, how can man be free to choose? This problem has long held a powerful fascination for the religious mind. In mediaeval Jewish thought the problem is known as that of *yedi'ah* ('knowledge', i.e. God's foreknowledge) and *beḥirah* ('choice', i.e. human freedom to choose). It being generally acknowledged in Judaism that the doctrine of God's omniscience embraces the sure and certain knowledge by Him of all future events and it being generally accepted as axiomatic that human beings are free, at least within limits, to pursue good and reject evil, the problem arises of how both beliefs can be mutually compatible and simultaneously held. If, long before a particular man is born, God knows to the last detail and with complete certainty all the deeds that man will perform during his lifetime, how can that man be free to do otherwise? To deny God's foreknowledge seems to suggest ignorance and limitation in God and hence appears to be incompatible with God's utter perfection. To deny human freedom, on the other hand, seems to make nonsense of the Jewish religion, which contains innumerable appeals to man to choose the good and which informs him that he will be rewarded for so doing, but punished if he does evil. From the middle ages down to the present the problem has been considered by a succession of Jewish thinkers.

It is widely held that the problem has been stated by Rabbi Akiba in the Mishnah (*Avot* 3:15). In its usual translation Akiba's saying reads: 'All is foreseen [*ha-kol tzafui*] and [or 'but'] freedom [of the will to behave as one chooses] is given [*ve-ha-reshut netunah*].' But it is by no means certain that the translation 'All is foreseen' is correct.

The Hebrew word *tzafui* may mean here 'seen' not 'foreseen', the significance of the saying being to call attention to the fact that God sees all that men do *now*, without referring at all to God's ability to see into the future.[1] The saying may be no more than an admonition to man to conduct himself worthily since God sees all his deeds, and since man has the freedom to choose well. It is, in any event, extremely unlikely that Akiba is referring to the problem of foreknowledge and free-will, which he seeks to solve by stating that both are true in a way we cannot grasp. The consideration of abstract metaphysical problems of this kind is foreign to the concrete, 'organic'[2] type of Rabbinic thought. Only by reading into it mediaeval modes of speculation can Akiba's saying yield the idea it is conventionally held to be postulating.

Maimonides, however, in his Commentary to the Mishnah, does understand Akiba to be saying that both beliefs are true: God has foreknowledge and yet man is free.[3] In his *Mishneh Torah* (*Teshuvah* 5:5) Maimonides writes that it is beyond the power of the human mind to grasp how God's foreknowledge can be reconciled with man's freedom of choice. Yet, even though the human mind cannot see how both beliefs can be true, it is necessary for the believer to accept both beliefs as true. Maimonides is not content to state it as a great mystery and leave it at that. He proceeds to demonstrate that the problem is due to the mistaken notion that we can fathom the mind of God, whereas, in reality, we are quite incapable of attaining any kind of comprehension of the divine mind. If God's knowledge were of the same order as human knowledge, albeit of infinitely greater degree, then indeed such knowledge of future events would be totally incompatible with human freedom.[4] The truth is, argues Maimonides, that God's knowledge is never of something external to Himself. Human cognition involves the person who knows, the process of knowing and the thing known, but in God Knower, knowledge and that which is known are one. This must be so since it cannot seriously be maintained that God acquires knowledge of that of which He was previously ignorant. God is a Knower, He is never a Learner. It follows from this that human beings can have as little comprehension of God's knowledge as they can have of God Himself since God is His knowledge and His knowledge Him. What Maimonides appears to be saying is that it is a logical impossibility for human foreknowledge to be compatible with human freedom but God's foreknowledge is part of God's knowledge in totality and this is identical with God Himself. We can have no 'knowledge' of God's knowledge, not even the 'knowledge' to declare it to be incompatible with human freedom.[5] 'Since this is so', concludes Maimonides, 'we are incapable of knowing how the Holy One, blessed be He, knows all creatures and all deeds but this we can know without any doubt, that a man's deeds depend on him alone, God neither influencing him nor compelling him to do that which he does.'

R Abraham Ibn David of Posquierès (d. 1198), the *Raabad*, in his stricture to this section of the *Mishneh Torah*, writes:

Says Abraham: This author did not follow the practice of sages, according to which no man should embark on an enterprise he cannot bring to a successful conclusion. He began by raising problems but left the problems unsolved, falling back on faith. It would have been better for him to have left the unsophisticated in their innocence without introducing doubt into their minds, perhaps causing them to entertain heretical thoughts for the time being. Even though there is no completely convincing solution to this problem, it is right to suggest here some kind of answer. So I say: If a man's virtue or his wickedness depended on the decree of the Creator we would then be obliged to say that His knowledge is His decree and then, indeed, the problem would have been extremely severe. As it is, the Creator has surrendered His power to control man's life by giving this power to man himself. Consequently, God's foreknowledge is not determinative but should rather be compared to the knowledge the astrologers have, who know by external means what will happen to this or that person. It is well known that the Creator has made every event, great or small, depend on the stars but, at the same time, He endowed man with reason to help him escape the fate decreed by the stars and from this results man's capacity to be virtuous or wicked. The Creator knows the force of the star and its times so that He knows whether man will possess sufficient power of reason to enable him to escape from the fate decreed by the star. Such knowledge is not determinative. But all this is really worthless.

Raabad accuses Maimonides of falling back on faith. But, if faith is the only solution, why raise the philosophical problem at all? As we have noted, however, Maimonides does offer a solution, by examining what is involved when we speak of God's knowledge. Maimonides does not simply say, as *Raabad* accuses, that we cannot see how foreknowledge and freedom are compatible but that we must believe by faith that somehow they are. Maimonides rather says that by philosophical analysis of the whole concept of God's foreknowledge we must arrive, by reason not by faith, at the conclusion that the problem is really a pseudo-problem in that it proceeds by postulating in God a knowledge that is akin to human knowledge. *Raabad*'s own solution is that God does not decree beforehand how a man must behave. To be sure, God does know beforehand how man will behave but such knowledge is not determinative. *Raabad*, unlike Maimonides, is a believer in astrology. He adopts the standard mediaeval view that man's general fate is determined by the stars but holds, since Judaism considers man to be free to choose the good, God has endowed man with reason, that is with the skill and talent to escape from the domination of the stars in those areas where his choice has moral significance. God does know beforehand whether in each particular instance man's reasoning powers will be strong enough to enable him to escape the fate decreed by the stars but this kind of knowledge is not determinative. *Raabad* concludes, nevertheless, that his attempted solution is really worthless; evidently because it is extremely difficult to see how certain foreknowledge, even of the kind *Raabad* postulates, can fail to be ultimately determinative.

Gersonides (1288–1344), who holds that if logical contradiction is to be avoided then either belief in God's foreknowledge or belief in human freedom requires qualification, adopts the very radical solution that God does not, in fact, know beforehand the particular choices man will make.[6] God knows all there is to know but if man is really free to choose, then, by definition, the actual choices he makes are unknowable before he makes them and this cannot fall under the scope of divine omniscience. It is not to ascribe ignorance to God to say that He does not know that which, by definition, is not knowledge. Gersonides makes the bold claim that his view alone makes sense of the Biblical passages which refer to man's freedom but which imply that his choice is not known to God beforehand. God does know the future in a general sense. He knows all the possibilities open to man and all the various results of particular choices. He does not know which particular choice man will make in each instance. No other representative Jewish thinker in the middle ages has been prepared to qualify so drastically the doctrine of divine omniscience. Theologically this reduces God's power to such an extent that the Supreme Being of Gersonides' scheme would not be recognized by the majority of believers as the God in whom they believe. Husik,[7] discussing Gersonides' view, says that it 'is surely very bold as theology, we might almost say it is a theological monstrosity.'

Hasdai Crescas (1340–1416), like Gersonides, believes[8] that it is logically impossible to maintain both that God has complete foreknowledge and that human beings are completely free, but, unlike Gersonides, Crescas is unwilling to limit God's foreknowledge in any way and consequently finds his way out of the dilemma by limiting human freedom. For Crescas, man is not fated to choose a particular act but it is determined, none the less by virtue of God's foreknowledge that he will, in fact, choose it. Man's choice is guided by the promise of reward for doing good and the threat of punishment for doing evil. Thus what is determined by God's foreknowledge is the whole process by means of which man arrives at his particular choices. There would be no justice in God granting reward to the righteous and punishing the wicked if rewards were in the nature of gifts for virtuous living and punishments were deprivations for evil living. Rewards and punishments are only the means by which a man is spurred on to lead a virtuous life and to reject a vicious life, operating as cause and effect. Crescas is fully aware of the difficulties inherent in his solution. He discusses why, since every human act is determined by God's foreknowledge, a distinction is made in Jewish law between voluntary acts, for which there is reward and punishment, and involuntary acts. Crescas tries hard to fit the distinction into his scheme. There is no point in rewarding or punishing acts done under compulsion since the whole purpose of reward and punishment, as Crescas has argued, is to influence man's choice. It can hardly be said that Crescas has offered an adequate solution to the problem. Alone of the mediaeval Jewish thinkers, Crescas prefers the determinist position.

Isaac b. Sheshet Perfet (1326–1408), the *Ribash*, in a Responsum[9] on the study of philosophy, is severely critical of Gersonides' solution. In another Responsum,[10] the *Ribash* replies to the question addressed to him by Amram of Oran, who wished to know how the opinion of the *Raabad*, which the *Ribash* does not attack, differs from that of Gersonides, which he does attack. The *Ribash* has no difficulty in distinguishing between the two views. Gersonides holds that God does not, in fact, know beforehand how man will choose in each particular instance. This cannot be correct, says the *Ribash*, since presumably He does know the particular acts once they have been performed (otherwise how can He reward virtue and punish vice) and it would follow, if Gersonides is correct, that God acquires knowledge of which He had previously been ignorant, which is a theological impossibility. *Raabad*, on the other hand, holds that God does know beforehand the particular choices of man but that His foreknowledge is not determinative. *Ribash* notes that *Raabad* is himself less than satisfied with his solution. *Ribash* then attempts a solution of his own. If it were simply the bare act that man performs that is known beforehand to God then, indeed, man would not be free. What God knows beforehand is not the act on its own but the act together with man's free choice to perform it. God knows beforehand how man will choose in his freedom. It is not the foreknowledge that determines the choice but the choice which determines, as it were, the foreknowledge. God knows beforehand how man will choose in his freedom so that man is completely free to choose. But, while *Ribash* seems to think that this is the best and most adequate solution to the problem, it is no real solution since the difficulty remains, as with *Raabad*, how can God's foreknowledge fail to be determinative.

Simeon b. Zemah Duran (1361–1444), in his Commentary to the Mishnah of Rabbi Akiba,[11] spells out the problem and Maimonides' solution. Duran writes:

According to this explanation the great problem arises to which the Gentiles have addressed themselves. This is, if God knows beforehand how man will behave, how can man be free since the divine foreknowledges the deed eventually carried out and it is impossible to change it? Consequently, there are two opinions among them on this question. The first is that God has no knowledge of what man will do and man is entirely free to do as he chooses. This is the opinion of the Greek sages but not of our sages of blessed memory who say:[12] How do we know God knows what will be in the future? Because Scripture says, 'And this people will arise and go awhoring' (Deuteronomy 31:16). The second opinion is that man has no freedom of choice and all is determined by the decree of the Creator. This is the opinion of the Arabic sages (of the Ashariya sect) who believe in determinism. Such an opinion is contrary to our Torah, which says, 'Choose life, therefore' (Deuteronomy 31:19). Man cannot be commanded to choose unless he is free so to do. Our teacher Moses [Maimonides], of blessed memory, rules that God does know the future beforehand but this knowledge has no coercive power over man. Although, as far as our knowledge is concerned, such a thing is impossible, God's knowledge is not like our knowledge, there being no point of comparison between them, since God and His knowledge are one and the same. Just as He is incomprehensible to us and we cannot know His nature, so, too, His knowledge is beyond our comprehension.

Thus Duran accepts that Maimonides is not simply throwing up his hands in despair but is offering a solution, albeit one that we cannot fathom, or, rather, is pointing out that the problem is not a real problem because we can say as little about God's knowledge as about His nature.

Yom Tov Lippmann Heller (1579–1654), in his famous Commentary to the Mishnah, *Tosafot Yom Tov*, in the section on Rabbi Akiba's saying, defends Maimonides against the stricture of *Raabad*. The latter criticizes Maimonides for raising an extremely difficult problem for faith without providing a solution. Maimonides, says Heller, simply follows Rabbi Akiba, who similarly provides no solution, his intention being to teach that the solution, as Maimonides states, is beyond man's ability to grasp. Heller quotes in this connection the well-known Commentary to *Avot*, entitled *Midrash Shemuel*, by Samuel b. Isaac Uceda (sixteenth century), which invokes the mystical idea of the Eternal Now to solve the problem. God does not see *beforehand* what man will do in the future. God sees all future acts of man being done *now*. If A sees B performing an act now, the fact that A sees B doing that act obviously does not interfere in any way with B's freedom to do it. This is how God sees all acts, future as well as past and present, since God is not in time but beyond time. Moses Almosnino (d.*c.* 1580) is quoted as suggesting that this idea is implied in what Maimonides says. When Maimonides seeks to distinguish, in this connection, between God's knowledge and human knowledge, this is precisely what he means. God's knowledge is never of the future since God is beyond time and His knowledge is always of the *present*. The reason we have difficulty in reconciling God's foreknowledge with human freedom is because we are incapable of grasping how God's knowledge can always be in the *present*. This is because, as human beings, we are bound by the time process. That is why Maimonides reminds us that in the nature of the case we cannot have any comprehension of God's knowledge. It is, of course, more than a little unlikely that this is what Maimonides means. Certainly there is no reference anywhere else in the writings of Maimonides to the mystical Eternal Now.[13]

The Moroccan Kabbalist, Hayyim Ibn Atar (1696–1743), attempts a solution of his own in his Commentary to the Pentateuch, *Or ha-Ḥayyim*.[14] Ibn Atar's ideas are clothed in mystical language and are obscure, but what he seems to be saying is that there can, indeed, be no human freedom where there is divine foreknowledge. In order to give man his freedom God voluntarily relinquishes His foreknowledge. Ibn Atar appears to hold that God's omniscience is not compromised by his voluntary surrender of His foreknowledge since it is voluntary. Moreover, Ibn Atar continues, God does not surrender His foreknowledge so far as the deeds of the righteous are concerned, from which it follows that man's good deeds are not performed in complete freedom and he deserves no reward for them. The righteous have grounds to protest God's rewarding them for their good deeds but 'no one complains against his own interest'. This is a very curious theory of religious determinism for the righteous and freedom for the wicked. Ibn Atar claims that Maimonides is saying the same thing. It is impossible for man to surrender his knowledge since self-induced ignorance is a contradiction in terms. But what is impossible for man is possible for God in His omnipotence. Again, it is hardly likely that Maimonides shares the views of Ibn Atar and, judging by Maimonides' general stance, he would have been greatly shocked by them.

A full-scale treatment of the problem is found in the work *'Amud ha-'Avodah*[15] by the Hasidic master Baruch of Kossov (d. 1795). Baruch cleverly reads Maimonides' views into the verse:

> Why sayest thou, O Jacob,
> And speakest, O Israel:
> 'My way is hid from the Lord,
> And my judgement is passed over from my God.'
> Hast thou not known? Hast thou not heard
> That the everlasting God, the Lord,
> The Creator of the ends of the earth,
> Fainteth not, neither is weary?
> His discernment is past searching out. (Isaiah 40:27–8)

That is to say, Jacob says, either my way is hid from the Lord (i.e. God has no foreknowledge) or my judgement is passed over from my God (i.e. man is not free and cannot, therefore, be judged for his deeds). To this the prophet replies, as does Maimonides, that God's discernment is past searching out (i.e. we are incapable of comprehending the great mystery since God's knowledge is beyond all human comprehension). Baruch quotes the saying:[16]

> A fool is a sage in his own eyes,
> A fool is a sage in his own eyes.

The first sentence should be read as it stands. The second should be read, 'A fool in his own eyes – is a sage', the sage seeing himself as a fool. Both sentences imply that the truly wise know that they do not know.

Baruch proceeds to discuss which type of unbelief is the more serious, denial that God has foreknowledge or denial that man is free. At first glance, he observes, it would seem that to deny God's foreknowledge is worse, touching as it does on the doctrine of God's complete perfection and imposing limits on God's powers. Yet, on deeper reflection, Baruch continues, it can be seen that it is worse to deny human freedom. The man who denies human freedom will eventually reject all religion and all religious doctrine, including the belief in God's foreknowledge. By denying human freedom, one would be bound to deny the truth of the Torah since the Torah appeals constantly to man as being capable of free choice. The result will be that such an unbeliever will give up his study of the Torah. But the man who believes in human freedom, though he denies God's foreknowledge, will continue to study the Torah and this very study will eventually convince him of the truth that God does have foreknowledge. As his mind becomes more mature through his studies he will discover how solutions are found to what seem to be insoluble problems so that, as Maimonides says, although he will never know the answer to this particular theological problem (of how God's foreknowledge can be reconciled with human freedom), yet he will no longer be tempted to deny that God has foreknowledge simply because the solution to the problem is beyond his grasp. This, claims Baruch, is the meaning of the idea mentioned in the Midrash[17] where God is made to say, 'Would that they had forsaken Me but kept My Torah, for the light therein will restore them to the good.' It is preferable that they give up belief in God's foreknowledge for the time being, but keep His Torah, rather than continue to believe in God's foreknowledge but deny human freedom and eventually give up the study of the Torah.

In an earlier work,[18] Baruch has a lengthy excursus on the problem. Here he takes issue with two earlier attempts, by Moses Alshekh (d.*c.* 1593) and Immanuel Hai Ricchi (1688–1743), at solving the problem. Alshekh, as expounded by Baruch, puts forward the idea that God's foreknowledge is so subtle and infinitely refined that it can have no influence on man's free choice. Baruch gives the illustration of the lever which can lift huge loads when operated by a human being yet the one who invented the lever could not lift these loads merely by thinking of the lever's operations. This, of course, does nothing to solve the problem. If God's foreknowledge is really certain, why does it not determine man's choice, infinitely subtle though that knowledge is? Baruch evidently does not see this as an objection but has another objection we shall note presently.

Hai Ricchi's solution is basically the same as that of Ibn Atar noted earlier. God surrenders His foreknowledge in order that man should have freedom of choice and all things are possible for God, including the surrender of His foreknowledge. Baruch demolishes both solutions, those of Alshekh and Hai Ricchi, on the basis of the verse, 'And also, behold, he cometh forth to meet thee, and when he seeth thee, he will be glad in his heart' (Exodus 4:14). Here God tells Moses that his brother Aaron will come out to meet him and Aaron will rejoice that Moses has been chosen by God. Now, argues Baruch, the clear implication of this is that Aaron exercised his free choice in rejoicing at the good news that Moses had been chosen, even though God knew of it beforehand and told it to Moses beforehand. Here, neither Alshekh's solution nor that of Hai Ricchi applies since here God's foreknowledge was expressed in speech to Moses (and was not, therefore, so subtle that it could have no effect on human conduct) and there was no surrender of the divine foreknowledge. Baruch proceeds to elaborate on the Eternal Now solution, as found in Heller, Uceda and Almosnino, with elaborations of his own. The division of time into past, present and future is due to the workings of the human mind, but for the mind of God past, present and future are seen in a single glance, as it were. God always sees man acting 'now' with his free choice. Since we are involved in the time process we cannot grasp adequately this tremendous idea, which is why Maimonides notes that the solution is beyond the grasp of the human mind.

Another Hasidic master to deal with the problem is the anti-rationalist thinker Zevi Elimelech of Dynow (1785–1841). Zevi Elimelech was a life-long opponent of the Mendelssohnian Enlightenment, considering it dangerous to faith. A problem such as ours, to which there is no solution, attracted the author, providing him with ammunition in his attack upon 'reason'. Here, at least, he argues, human reasoning is sterile and only simple faith can be our guide. In his *Beney Yissakhar*,[19] Zevi Elimelech advances the argument that God has intentionally concealed the solution to our problem so that men should believe solely by faith. Those who follow the good life solely because their reason so dictates cannot excuse their sins by saying, 'Because of God's foreknowledge we are not free', since their sole guide, human reasoning, is powerless to solve the contradiction. Since they hold that they are free because their reason so tells them, they are not entitled to claim immunity from punishment on the grounds of faith. But the Jewish people, the faithful believers, know that they are free only because of their faith (which alone guides them and helps them to live with the contradiction between their freedom and God's foreknowledge). Since their very freedom is accepted by them on faith, it is right that God shows them mercy and treats them as if they had not sinned in full freedom. Or, as Zevi Elimelech puts it,

> God in His mercy and in His desire to justify His people, behaves in His relationship with them in His quality of mercy, higher than reason. For reason is justice; it is just and reasonable that those who disobey the king's commands of their own free choice should be punished. But in connection with this very matter of reward and punishment, God has concealed even from the wise how punishment can be justified for sins committed as a result of bad choice since God knows it all beforehand. But the children of Israel believe in it by virtue of the Torah, the Torah of mercy, higher than reason. It follows automatically that even from the point of view of justice, it is only right for their sins to be pardoned and for mercy to be shown to them.

Thus Israel deserves to be punished for sins only because it is so stated in the Torah, not because it is 'reasonable'. But in the realm of the Torah all is mercy and pardon. By concealing the solution to our problem God provides, so to speak, a built-in excuse for those who worship Him in faith.

One of the most profound Hasidic thinkers, Aaron of Starosselje (1766–1826), discusses our problem in terms of his own Hasidic philosophy. Aaron belonged to the *Ḥabad* school of Hasidism, a school which draws a distinction between man's view of the universe and, as it were, God's view of the universe. In his treatment of our problem,[20] Aaron appears to be saying that the difficulty is caused by our failure to appreciate this distinction. From our point of view, in which the universe is seen as enjoying an existence independent of, or at least separate from, God, there is no foreknowledge and man is therefore free. Time is real from our point of view. There is past, present and future.

However, we must not think of God knowing in the past what will happen in the future. In Rabbi Akiba's Mishnah, it is said not that God *knows* but that God *sees*. The real problem is not that of foreknowledge versus free-will, but rather of the very notion of *fore*knowledge. Such a temporal term has meaning only from our point of view. To ask how the idea of foreknowledge can be present if there is no time sequence at all from God's point of view is to do no more than to restate the problem of how there can be a finite universe at all if God is all. The truth is that we do not know and cannot possibly grasp this mystery. Aaron calls it a *pelé*, a 'marvel', impossible for the human mind to comprehend.

The novelty in Aaron's thought (while basically a variation of the Eternal Now solution) is that he sees the problem of foreknowledge versus free-will in terms of the wider problem of the very existence of a finite universe. This latter problem is, indeed, an insoluble mystery, 'higher than reason' in Aaron's terminology. But once this mystery has been accepted by an act of faith, there is no further problem of foreknowledge versus free-will, for in speaking of foreknowledge we are speaking of that which really belongs to the category of God's point of view, whereas in speaking of free will we speak from our point of view. From God's point of view, 'before' creation, one cannot speak of 'knowledge' at all. At this stage, one we are forbidden to contemplate, all divisions, including the very distinction between good and evil, are in the category of one simple force. It is only when the divine light is progressively screened so that the finite universe appears to enjoy an existence separate from God that the detailed divisions come into being. All the divisions exist, as it were, in potentiality, from the beginning, but it is only as a result of man's free choice that these become actualized or revealed.

Two more recent thinkers of the traditional school who consider our problem at length are: Meir Simhah Kagan (1843–1926),[21] Rabbi of Dvinsk in Latvia, and Joseph Laib Bloch (1860–1930), Rabbi and Head of the Yeshivah in Telz, Lithuania.[22] Meir Simhah Kagan first examines and rejects as unsatisfactory the various solutions to the problems advanced by earlier thinkers, and then remarks that we are obliged to fall back on Maimonides' statement that we cannot know the answer because God's knowledge is really God Himself and of God's nature we can have no comprehension whatsoever. To ask the question is akin to asking what is the true nature of God. This does not mean, as *Raabad* suggests in his critique of Maimonides, that Maimonides has been unwise in stating a problem and then replying that there is no solution. Maimonides is not, in fact, saying that there is no solution. Maimonides is saying, rather, that the solution, bound up as it is with the nature of God, is utterly beyond the scope of the human mind. Meir Simhah points to certain mathematical problems that are insoluble, so that even in this world the idea of an insoluble problem is logically coherent.

Joseph Laib Bloch refers to Midrashic statements (which he takes literally), which state that certain prophets not only foresaw the future in broad strokes, but the particular acts of yet unborn individuals as well. Bloch finds such statements exceedingly puzzling. We can accept Maimonides' argument that somehow, in a way we cannot understand, God's foreknowledge can be compatible with human freedom of choice. But the prophets were human beings and their foreknowledge of particular events, as stated in the Midrashic passages, was a purely human foreknowledge, existing in a human, not a divine, mind. It is extremely difficult to understand how this human foreknowledge can be compatible with human free-will.

Bloch, too, invokes the idea of the Eternal Now. He refers to the Kabbalistic view that time and space have no independent existence and claims that modern philosophers (is he referring to Kant?) have called attention to the purely cognitive nature of space and time. Bloch writes:

> We know that the whole idea of time only enjoys existence according to our perception. But from the point of view of the highest reality there is no time in the sense of past, present and future but all is in the eternal 'present'. It follows that, in reality, God's foreknowledge does not precede man's free choice. It is rather that they both take place simultaneously. Relative to our mode of apprehension we are obliged to depict it as if all human beings have been created from the beginning and all deeds have been carried out and in that very moment each human being has chosen his way of life, so that knowledge never precedes choice. Rather, it is that whoever will be righteous in the future has already chosen the righteous way from the beginning. It follows that there is no contradiction between God's and human choice. Such a contradiction only appears to us as real because we are bound by time and so experience God's knowledge as prior to human choice. But in the 'eternal present' it is quite possible for both knowledge and free will to exist simultaneously. Understand this!

All this concerns God's foreknowledge. But what of the question Bloch raises concerning the foreknowledge of the prophets as stated in the Midrash? How can this be at all compatible with human free-will? Although he does take the Midrashic statements literally, Bloch argues that these statements do not mean that the prophets have the same kind of foreknowledge as God. That would be sheer impossibility. What the Midrashic statements imply is that the foreknowledge of the prophets is part of God's creation. The prophet gazes into the future to see the whole of God's plan unfolding and in this sense he foresees the deeds of a particular individual in particular circumstances. None the less, that individual can change his destiny, as seen by the prophetic vision, through the exercise of his free choice. The prophet's foreknowledge is not of the same order as God's foreknowledge. It is conditional. What the prophet sees is the unfolding of the divine plan as determined by the natural order implanted by God. The man who strives to be righteous can elevate himself above the whole natural order, including the events which the prophets foresaw.

All the thinkers we have mentioned either belong to the middle ages or are completely traditionalist in outlook and so operate within mediaeval categories of thought. The problem does not seem to have bothered modern Jewish thinkers at all. There are no doubt a number of reasons for this. First, there is the tendency among some modernists to think of God in terms of process or as the impersonal Ground of Being or the force that makes for righteousness. The God of these thinkers is not a Being with knowledge and will. If the problem of free-will is to be discussed by these thinkers it must be along the general philosophical lines of determinism versus free-will, not of foreknowledge versus free will. An 'It' has neither foreknowledge nor any other kind of knowledge. Even those thinkers who see no reason for abandoning the traditional concept of God tend to be more pragmatic than theoretical, concerned far more with the implications of theology for man's spiritual life than with abstract considerations regarding the divine nature. Again, both the existentialists and the linguistic philosophers have a deep mistrust of metaphysics in general so that our problem becomes irrelevant 'cosmic talk' for the existentialists and a pseudo-problem for the linguistic analysts, who would presumably argue that the language used in our speculation cannot be 'cashed' and is therefore logically bankrupt. Those of us who still believe in the traditional doctrine of God – i.e. of God as a Person, as more than a *He*, to be sure, but not an *It* – and who still wish to see religious truth grounded in reason, still find the problem not only fascinating in itself but relevant to our religious quest. We might fall back on an elaboration of the Eternal Now idea, especially as a result of more recent investigations into the paranormal and the possible ability even of humans to transcend the time barriers. But we are on safer grounds in following the example of Maimonides and the idea put forward by Aaron of Starosselje. As believers we affirm what is, after all, the greatest mystery of all, that this finite universe, full of darkness and error as well as light and truth, is the creation of the All-good, Omnipotent and Omniscient. In a way we cannot see in this life, God, in the language of the Lurianic Kabbalah, has withdrawn in order to give man a degree of autonomy. In this area, as in others, it is very hard to believe in God but it is harder still not to believe in Him.

CHAPTER II

Immortality

Ultimately the question of the significance of the individual in Judaism can best be discussed by considering his part in the Jewish eschatological scheme. What has to be examined in this chapter is how Jewish teaching treats the doctrine of the immortality of the individual soul. In this area much is highly speculative but it is possible to trace briefly the history of the doctrine from the Biblical period onwards.

The virtual silence on the whole question of individual immortality in the Bible has often been noted. As Salo Baron remarks:[1]

> Entire libraries could be filled with writings on the Old Testament doctrine of the Hereafter, even more than ordinarily contrasting with the paucity of the biblical statements themselves. This is not altogether surprising when one considers the enormous role this doctrine was to play in the subsequent world outlook of Judaism and its daughter religions.

Of the two great civilizations which formed the background to the Biblical texts, the Babylonian and the Egyptian, there was a marked difference on the doctrine of the Hereafter. In the Babylonian religion in its official aspects the doctrine occupied a very secondary place, while in the Egyptian religion the doctrine was prominent, as can be seen from the evidence of the tombs filled with objects the deceased would need.[2] As W. B. Emery puts it,[3] the Egyptians believed that 'you could take it with you'. Kaufmann[4] has suggested convincingly that the doctrine was so bound up, in the ancient religions of the Near East, with the realm of the gods, to which the dead were allowed access, that the monotheistic authors of the Bible tended consciously to ignore the whole notion. It is imprecise to say that the idea of the immortality of the soul is unknown in Biblical religion. It is known but is not brought into association with the official religion.

For all that, the supposed conscious silence of the Bible needs some degree of qualification. The punishment of *karet*, being cut off, may possibly refer to the fate of the soul in the Hereafter.[5] The frequent references to Sheol[6] as the abode of the dead, though seeming to denote a shadowy, vague mode of existence, do seem to imply that there is some kind of survival after death. On a surface reading, at least, of the story of the Witch of Endor (1 Samuel 28:13–19), Samuel was brought from the realm of the dead, implying that he had his abode there. When the patriarch Jacob begs Joseph not to bury him in Egypt, he says, 'But when I sleep with my fathers, thou shalt carry me out of Egypt, and bury me in their burying-place' (Genesis 47:29–30); the expression 'sleeping' or 'lying' with the fathers is distinct from 'and bury me in their burying-place', seeming to suggest that this expression denotes not burial in the ancestral tomb but a state after the death of the body. The same expression is used of Abraham (Genesis 25:8), and he was not buried in his father Terah's tomb. When the prophet Jeremiah addresses the matriarch Rachel (Jeremiah 31:14–15), poetic though the passage is, he implies that Rachel is still alive and can hear him. The prohibition of necromancy (Deuteronomy 18:10–11) similarly implies, on a surface reading at least, that the dead are there to be contacted by the living, although the attempted contact is forbidden. The most explicit reference to the Hereafter is in the book of Daniel (12:2–3):

> And many of those that sleep in the dust of the earth shall awake, some to everlasting life, and some to shame and everlasting contempt. And they that be wise shall shine as the brightness of the firmament; and they that turn many unto righteousness as the stars for ever and ever.

Daniel, however, it is the consensus of scholarly opinion, is a late book dating from a time when Jewish eschatology had been more fully developed. By the time of the Maccabees, when young men were being martyred for their faith and the older doctrine of reward and punishment in this life no longer seemed plausible, the doctrine of the Hereafter came into its own.[7] According to many scholars the book of Daniel was, in fact, compiled at this time. According to the Rabbinic tradition,[8] the Sadducees held that 'there is only one world', this one, while the Pharisees believed in the World to Come. There is a certain ambiguity about the term the World to Come, which can and usually does refer to the world after the resurrection of the dead but can also refer to the immortality of the soul. Josephus tells us[9] that the Sadducees rejected the belief in the immortality of the soul.[10] The belief in the immortality of the soul is very strong in 'The Wisdom of Solomon' (first century CE):

> The souls of the righteous are in the hand of God,
> And there shall no torment touch them.
> In the sight of the unwise they seemed to die;
> And their departure was taken to be their hurt,
> And their journeying away from us to be their ruin;
> But they are in peace.
> For though they be punished in the sight of men,
> Yet is their hope full of immortality. (3:1–4)

On the other hand, there is no clear belief in immortality in Ben Sira (*c.* 200 BCE) or in the book of Tobit. But again the belief is very strong in II Maccabees 7:36 and 12:43–4 (*c.* 60 BCE). On Philo, H. A. Wolfson[11] observes:

> Throughout his writings Philo speaks of the immortality of the soul rather than the resurrection of the body. No direct or indirect reference to the resurrection as distinguished from immortality is ever made by him, though the belief in resurrection was common among the Egyptians of his own native country, and though it is also mentioned in the Sibylline oracles. But it is quite evident that all the references to the resurrection of his time were understood by him as being only a figurative way of referring to immortality.

If we turn to the Talmudic literature, the literature with the greatest influence on subsequent Jewish doctrine, the main emphasis is on the resurrection. Despite suggestions to the contrary, the term '*Olam ha-Ba*, 'The World to Come', in this literature usually refers to the resurrection of the dead *here on earth*, not to the fate of the soul after the death of the body.[12] Both ideas, that of the resurrection and that of immortality of the soul, had been accepted and amalgamated by the Rabbinic period, though, as has been noted, the former idea is the more prominent. However, there are passages in the literature in which the term '*Olam ha-Ba* does seem to refer to immortality – this, for instance:[13]

> Rabbi Eleazar b. R Zadok said: To what can the righteous in this world be compared, to a tree, the trunk of which stands in a place of purity with its branches inclining towards a place of impurity. Once the branches have been cut off the whole tree stands in a place of purity. In the same way, the Holy One, blessed be He, brings sufferings upon the righteous in this world in order for them to inherit the World to Come ['*Olam ha-Ba*].

There are numerous references in this literature to the reward of the righteous in *Gan Eden*, 'The Garden of Eden',[14] and the punishment of the wicked in Gehinnom,[15] but these, too, are sufficiently opaque to allow considerable room for free interpretation among the later Jewish teachers.

In a famous Talmudic passage[16] there is a debate whether the dead know what is happening on earth, implying that their souls are in 'Heaven' (this term is not, however, used for the abode of the souls in the Rabbinic literature) and the same applies to the references to the scholars in the 'Academy on High' (*metivta de-rakia'*).[17]

For all the references in the Talmudic literature, it was not until the middle ages that attempts were made to devise a systematic Jewish eschatology. Among the mediaeval Jewish philosophers, the doctrine of the resurrection was never abandoned but the emphasis was undoubtedly on the immortality of the soul.

According to Saadia Gaon, in his *Emunot ve-De'ot*, 'Beliefs and Opinions', there are no pre-existent souls. The soul is created simultaneously with the body. When the body dies the soul remains in a state of separation until the number of souls to be created has been reached, when the soul is reunited with the body and both body and soul are rewarded or punished according to their conduct while they were united on earth.[18] The purpose of God placing the soul in the body is for the soul to acquire greater luminosity through obedience to God's commandments despite the hindrances here on earth. Sin, on the other hand, has the effect of making the soul's substance turbid. The sojourn of the soul on earth causes it to be tested and refined. Only such a refined soul is capable of attaining to eternal life and the body is the instrument the soul uses to achieve its lofty final aim. As for the question why could God not have endowed the soul with the power to *act* without having to use the body as its instrument, this is akin to asking why the soul is a soul and not a body. It is the very nature of the soul, separate in its substance from matter, that it can obey God's commandments in the material world only through the physical body.[19] When a man is about to die, the angel of death appears to him, at which dreaded appearance he shudders and his soul departs. All souls, after the death of the body, are stored up to await their reunification with the body at the time of the resurrection and retribution. Pure souls are kept on high under the Throne of Glory. Turbid souls are fated to wander aimlessly below. Until the decomposition of the body the soul has no fixed abode and it suffers from the contemplation of the body's fate just as former inhabitants of a house now in ruins are aggrieved at seeing what has become of the house they had loved. This is the meaning of the Talmudic[20] saying that the worms are as painful to a corpse as a needle thrust into living flesh.[21] Saadia, incidentally, rejects belief in the transmigration of souls, which he considers to be a foreign importation into Judaism.[22]

Saadia[23] insists that Jews ('all our nation') have always believed in the resurrection of the dead. If Jews believe in *creation ex nihilo* there are no special difficulties in belief in the resurrection of the dead. According to Saadia, there will be two resurrections: the first, for the virtuous of Israel in the Messianic age, the second for all men who will be judged in the World to Come, identified by Saadia with the resurrection. After the first resurrection, men will still eat, drink and marry as before, but eventually they will be transferred to a place in which there will be no bodily activities such as eating and drinking. They will be in the state Moses occupied when he went on high (Exodus 34:28). In the first resurrection, all virtuous Jews and Jewish sinners who have repented will enjoy life in this world. At the second resurrection the World to Come will be ushered in for all mankind. Thus for Saadia the World to Come (after the second resurrection) is totally different from the worldly state Jews will enjoy at the first resurrection. Those still alive at the first resurrection will live for a very long time (five hundred years, says Saadia) but, since death has been decreed on mankind, they will eventually die to be resurrected at the time of the second resurrection.[24] Saadia continues[25] with much speculation on the nature of reward and punishment in the Hereafter. He believes that Judaism teaches eternal punishment for some sinners, though he qualifies this somewhat by speaking of degrees of intensity and by identifying Gehinnom with a 'luminous substance'. In the Hereafter men will have many opportunities for serving God but the nature of this worship will be solely by means of human rational qualities, i.e. by contemplation and the acknowledgement of God.[26]

Saadia's views have been quoted at length as an illustration of the inevitable difficulties faced and hardly overcome in an attempt to impose system on material that has come down from many different ages and thinkers, including the pure speculations as well as what might be considered more or less precise theological formulations. Maimonides faces the same difficulties and reads, in fact, his own ideas into the sources.

Maimonides' doctrine of immortality is based on the Aristotelian view, in its Arabic garb, according to which only the part of man's intellect that he has acquired through the contemplation of metaphysical truths is immortal. The natural soul of man, that which keeps him alive and enables him to exist in the body, belongs, as in animals, to the body and ceases to function with the death of the body. Only the 'acquired soul' (*sekhel ha-nikneh*), which has become associated with the Active Intellect which comes from God, is immortal like its Source.[27] It will be seen why Maimonides has great difficulty with the traditional Jewish doctrine of the resurrection of the body. Maimonides makes no mention of the resurrection in his *Guide of the Perplexed*, though, among his thirteen principles of the Jewish faith, he does count belief in the resurrection,[28] albeit in a very perfunctory manner. Maimonides was consequently accused of denying the resurrection and was obliged to write his 'Treatise on the Resurrection' in order to defend his orthodoxy.[29] Here he argues that he does believe, as do other Jews, in the resurrection as a miracle God will perform but implies that the doctrine is secondary and states, moreover, that the resurrected dead will eventually return to dust, the soul alone (i.e. the 'acquired soul') being immortal. In his *Mishneh Torah*,[30] Maimonides identifies '*Olam ha-Ba* with the immortality of the soul and interprets all the Rabbinic references to the 'World to Come' as referring to that 'World', which, he remarks, is already here and is referred to as 'coming' only because this state cannot be attained while the soul is in the body. Saadia, too, as we have seen, refers to the death of the righteous still alive at the time of the first resurrection, but, for Saadia, the second resurrection is on earth and the resurrected bodies will live forever, whereas, for Maimonides, the resurrection of the dead on earth is only temporary. For Maimonides, then, the ultimate purpose of human existence is for the individual to gain the 'acquired soul' and thus gain immortality. For the same reason, Maimonides understands the Messianic age not as an end but as a means to the glorious end of immortality. Freed from the threat of war and other calamities, the sages will be able, in the Messianic age, to devote themselves to the philosophical reflection that will result in their soul's immortality.[31] Nahmanides, in his *Torat ha-Adam*,[32] takes strong issue with Maimonides, holding that '*Olam ha-Ba* refers to the world after the resurrection. It is the body that occupies '*Olam ha-Ba*, though it will be a subtle, refined body, not the murky body the soul inhabits in this life.

It can be seen that Maimonides' view is highly intellectual. Instead of the traditional, Rabbinic view that the way to inherit the World to Come is by obeying God's commands and living a moral and religious life, Maimonides has substituted the way of intellectual grasping of metaphysical truth, towards which the observance of the commandments are the means; important and essential means, to be sure, but means none the less. It has been jokingly remarked that evidently for Maimonides you cannot get to Heaven without a good degree in philosophy.

Maimonides[33] has his own understanding of the Talmudic description of the Hereafter attributed to the early third-century Babylonian teacher, Rav:[34] 'In the World to Come there is no eating nor drinking nor propagation nor business nor jealousy nor hatred nor competition, but the righteous sit with their crowns on their heads feasting on the brightness of the Shekhinah.' As we have seen, Maimonides understands the Talmudic references to '*Olam ha-Ba* as applying to the fate of the soul in the Hereafter. He is obliged, therefore, to interpret Rav's saying figuratively. When Rav says that the righteous 'sit', the meaning is that their souls are at rest; in a state of repose and tranquillity. The 'crowns' are the knowledge they had acquired in their lifetime on earth, which now becomes fully revealed and actualized.

In the Kabbalah, Rav's saying is similarly spiritualized. In a Zoharic passage[35] it is said that while there is no physical eating and drinking in the Hereafter the righteous do enjoy the spiritual food and drink of ever greater comprehension of divine truth, hence the references to the great banquet prepared for the righteous where they will imbibe the wine stored in the vat from the six days of creation. In another passage[36] the Zohar understands the 'crowns' on the heads of the righteous to be the crown of the holy spirit. In another passage[37] it is stated that the souls of the righteous become angels who sing God's praises and feast on the brightness of the Shekhinah.

The purpose of the soul's descent, the Zohar[38] states, is for the desire of the soul for God to be awakened from below, i.e. here on earth, so that when it returns to its Source on high a new harmony is restored in the Sefirotic realm. Without its probationary period on earth the soul is a cistern, into which water is poured from outside. After the soul has acquitted itself well, it ascends on high to become a fountain with water of its own. This passage seems to be the source of an idea expressed in the writings of Moshe Hayyim Luzzatto (1707–45), a religious genius and Kabbalist, said by some, because of his exquisite Hebrew style, to be the real father of modern Hebrew literature. Luzzatto develops the idea of what he calls 'bread of shame'.[39] God could have given man of His goodness without sending down the soul to inhabit the body. But then that goodness would be an unearned goodness, like the poor man who eats 'bread of shame' at the table of a rich man. By acquitting itself well in the body the soul makes the goodness its own and becomes Godlike in that God's goodness is integral to Him, so to speak.

Luzzatto's *Mesillat Yesharim* ('Path of the Upright') is a very popular manual of devotion, describing the steps on the ladder of saintliness.[40] In chapter one of this book, after stating the need for man to know why he has been created and what his purpose in life should be, Luzzatto says:

> Our Sages have taught us that man was created only to take delight in the Lord, and to feast on the brightness of His Shekhinah, for this is the true delight and the greatest of all pleasures. But the real place for such pleasure is the World to Come, which has been created for that very purpose. But this world is the way to attain that goal... Tempted [during this sojourn on earth] both by prosperity and by adversity, man is engaged in a severe battle. But if he is valorous and achieves the complete victory, he becomes the perfect man worthy to enjoy communion with his Creator. Then he will pass from the vestibule of this world into the palace to enjoy the light of Life. To the extent that a man subdues his evil inclination, keeps aloof from the things that prevent him from attaining the good, and endeavours to commune with God, to that extent is he certain to achieve the true life and rejoice in it.

Luzzatto's remarks here are an anticipation of Keats' 'this world is a vale of soul-making'.

So far we have been considering in this chapter ancient and mediaeval views on individual immortality. (Although Luzzatto lived in the eighteenth century, the historian Zunz rightly remarked that the Jewish middle ages lasted until the end of the eighteenth century.) Modern Jewish thinkers, it is often said, are this-worldly in outlook, either rejecting belief in individual immortality or being indifferent to it. Nowadays, it is also often said, the individual enjoys immortality through his works or his offspring or in the lives of those made better because he lived. This is really sleight of hand. No doubt the works and ideas and even the genes of a man live on after the death of his body, but so far as that individual is concerned none of these is 'he' in any significant understanding of the word. And it is simply not true that 'modern' thinkers have given up the idea of personal immortality. From the nineteenth century the Reform Movement in Judaism did give up the belief in the resurrection of the dead, removing references to this belief from their prayer books, but they substituted for it belief in the immortality of the soul. This return to Philo and, in a sense, also to Maimonides, can be observed among some of the Orthodox as well, who, similarly, prefer to stress the immortality of the soul rather than the resurrection of the dead, even while continuing to use the traditional vocabulary in their prayer books.[41] In any event, in this area especially, it can be seen how prominent the significance of the individual has been in Jewish thought from ancient times down to the present. While in other areas, the emphasis may have been on the group rather than the individual, in the doctrine of the Hereafter it is the individual soul that enjoys God forever.

A further question to be considered is how Jewish teachers conceived of eternal bliss for the individual soul. The study of the Torah having, for the Talmudic Rabbis, the highest religious value, it is natural that this activity is seen as continuing in the Yeshivah on High, the assembly of scholars debating and discussing the laws of the Torah as they did while on earth.[42] But there are also to be found Talmudic references to the individual experiencing Heavenly bliss in his individual uniqueness rather than as part of a group experience. In the very unusual tale about a visit to the next world,[43] it is told how R Joseph son of R Joshua b. Levi went into a trance[44] during which his soul entered the Heavenly realms. On his return to earth, R Joseph was asked by his father, 'What kind of world did you see?' R Joseph replied, 'I saw a topsy-turvey world. Those who are superior down here are inferior there and those inferior here are superior there.' 'Verily', the father responded, 'you saw a true world.' The father continued, 'And what about us?' (i.e. the scholars). 'We are there as we are here' (meaning, in all probability, that scholars have a true assessment of their status and there is consequently no need for their roles to be reversed up there). The son continued, 'I heard them saying, "Happy is he who comes here with his learning in his hand." And I heard them saying, "No one can stand in the compartment of the martyrs slain by the [Roman] Government."'

In an astonishing comment on this passage, Sherira Gaon (d. 1006) remarks:[45]

With regard to the superior ones being below and the inferior above, our master, light of our eyes, said in the name of R Joseph Gaon, who heard it from the great men of former times, that he [R Joseph son of R Joshua b. Levi] saw Mar Samuel [the famous third-century Babylonian teacher], teacher of R Judah, sitting [as a disciple] before R Judah because on one occasion R Judah rebuked his master. As we have learnt:[46] R Judah was sitting before Samuel when a woman came and cried out to him [Samuel] for help but he took no notice of her. Said R Judah: Does not the master agree that 'whoso stoppeth his ears at the cry of the poor, he also shall cry, but shall not be heard' (Proverbs 21:13).

The idea of special 'compartments' for the saints in the Hereafter is found in other Talmudic passages, in the following for example:[47]

Rabbah said in the name of R Johanan: the Holy One, blessed be He, will make seven canopies for every righteous man [in the Hereafter] as it is said: 'And the Lord will create over the whole habitation of Mount Zion, and over her assemblies, a cloud of smoke by day, and the shining of a flaming fire by night; for over all her glory shall be a canopy' (Isaiah 4:5). This teaches that the Holy One, blessed be He, will make for everyone a canopy corresponding to his honour. Why is smoke required in a canopy? R Hanina said: Because whoever is ungenerous to scholars in this world will have his eyes filled with smoke in the World to Come. Why is fire required in a canopy? R Hanina said: This teaches that each one will be burnt by the canopy of his fellow [i.e. in envy at the superior state of the other]. Alas for such shame. Alas for such reproach.

The Zohar develops this idea in its own mystical fashion when it states[48] that there are numerous 'places' (*atrin*) in the next world and each of the saints is allotted a place corresponding to his own spiritual stage. In that world, states the Zohar, there are various grades of illumination. Just as the spiritual illuminations of people differ in this life, so, too, they differ in the next world and each soul is put to shame (*ikhsif*) through the greater illumination enjoyed by its companion.[49]

In an appendage to the Mishnah,[50] R Joshua b. Levi observes that the Holy One, blessed be He, will cause each individual saint [*kol eḥad ve-eḥad*] to inherit three hundred and ten 'worlds', again stressing individual experience in separateness from the group. This saying is attributed in the Babylonian Talmud[51] to the Palestinian scholars in the name of Rava bar Mari and it is generally agreed by scholars that it did not appear originally in the Mishnah. As in the above-mentioned story, it would seem that the name of R Joshua b. Levi tended to be invoked when discussions of a mystical or other-worldly nature took place. The passage occurs at the end of the final tractate of the Mishnah and was obviously added in order to provide a 'happy ending'.

The following comment is found in the Midrash[52] on the verse, 'For man goeth to his long home' (Ecclesiastes 12:5). The Midrash plays on the Hebrew, translated as 'his long home', *le-vet 'olamo*, which means literally 'to his world's home'. Thus the Midrash, stressing the word 'his', states that each individual has his own special abode in the next world. 'It can be compared to a king who entered a province accompanied by generals, commanders and officers. Although they all entered through the same gate, each went and lodged in a place corresponding to his rank. Similarly, although all human beings experience death, each has a world for himself.' Whatever 'worlds' means in these contexts, it would appear that even when stressing individual experience this has somehow to be linked to the wider experience represented by the notion of a world or worlds.

In another Midrash[53] the idea is expressed even more emphatically. R Simeon b. Halafta came home before the Sabbath and found that there was no food for the day. He prayed to God and a precious stone dropped from Heaven. He sold the stone and bought with some of the money food for the Sabbath. When he told his wife how he had come by the food, she begged him to return the money, otherwise, she said, his table in the next world would lack all good things while the tables of his colleagues would be laden with them. When R Simeon reported on his wife's objection to R Judah the Prince, the latter said to him, 'Go tell your wife that if anything is lacking at your table I will replenish it from mine.' The wife protested, 'Does one saint see the other in the World to Come? Does not each of the saints have a world to himself?', and she quoted the verse in Ecclesiastes and the comment on it, as above. Whereupon R Simeon returned the money. With a touch of humour the passage concludes that for them to take it back was a greater miracle than for them to give it in the first place since 'up there' they give but do not take back.

In another Talmudic passage[54] there is this comment on the verse, 'God has made even the one as well as the other' (Ecclesiastes

7:14): 'Each person has two portions, one in the Garden of Eden and one in Gehinnom. The righteous man takes his own portion and his fellow's portion in the Garden of Eden. The wicked man takes his own portion and his fellow's portion in Gehinnom'; again the idea of an individual 'portion' of Heavenly bliss (and torment in Hell). Both ideas, that of group and individual experience, are given expression in the concluding passage of tractate *Ta'anit*[55] (another example of a saying added for the purpose of providing a 'happy ending' with the theme of the bliss of the saints in the Hereafter):

R Helbo said in the name of R Ulla of Bis, who said it in the name of R Eleazar: In the future the Holy One, blessed be He, will arrange a chorus for the saints in the Garden of Eden. He will sit among them and each of them will point at Him with his finger, as it is said, 'And it shall be said in that day: Lo, this is our God, for whom we waited, that he may save us; this is the Lord, for whom we waited, we will be glad and rejoice in His salvation' (Isaiah 25:9).

Both the mediaeval Jewish philosophers[56] and the mystics understand eternal bliss in the Hereafter in individualistic terms (though not necessarily exclusively so) at least so far as the mystics are concerned. The sixteenth-century Kabbalist Elijah de Vidas has a good deal to say on our theme in his guide to holy living, entitled *Reshit Ḥokhmah*, and where, on the basis of Zoharic passages, he refers to the Lower Gan Eden and the Higher Gan Eden. In the former, each of the saints is clothed in his own garment and there the saints can recognize one another as they do in this world.[57] De Vidas tells of a saint known as R Lapidot,[58] who testified to de Vidas' teacher, Moses Cordovero, about a dream which he had had in Upper Galilee in which the saint, R Judah Ibn Shushan, appeared to him with his face as bright as the sun and with the hairs of his head like flaming torches. He asked the saint to what virtue he attributed this splendour and the saint replied that it was all due to his capacity for silence since, all his life, he had uttered no vain words.

The Zohar[59] is quoted by de Vidas[60] to the effect that after seven days from his death a man's corpse begins to deteriorate and his soul speeds to its place on high and enters the Cave of Machpelah. There it 'sees what it sees and enters the place it enters' until it reaches the entrance to the Lower Gan Eden guarded by the Cherubim and the flaming sword. If the soul is worthy it is allowed to enter. But only the greatest of the saints, those who, during their lifetime on earth, had no worldly thoughts, are allowed to ascend, by means of a certain pillar, to the Higher Gan Eden.[61]

In the mystical diary kept by R Joseph Karo (1388–1575), author of the *Shulḥan 'Arukh*,[62] he records that his Heavenly mentor assured him that he would suffer martyrdom, after which all the saints in Gan Eden and the Shekhinah with them would come forth to meet him with songs and praises. Seven canopies had been provided for him, one higher than the other and within the seventh there would be seven rivers of fragrant balsam. There are further vivid and very concrete descriptions of the honours that will be paid to the saint, and the vision concludes:

> Afterwards a river of fire will gush forth and as you immerse yourself in it the fourteenth robe will be removed. As you emerge a precious white robe will be made ready for you to wear and Michael the high priest will be ready to bring up your soul to the Holy One, blessed be He. From this stage onwards permission has not been granted to describe what will transpire.

The references to the company of the saints and to the honours paid to the saint are very revealing. Even though ultimately the saint is alone with God with further description impossible, companionship evidently cannot be dispensed with in the earlier stages.

Hasidic thought, with its strong other-worldly thrust, naturally invited speculation on the fate of the individual soul in the Hereafter. Any inquiry into Hasidic thought is now assisted by the anthologies produced by M. S. Kasher,[63] though Kasher is too prone to see Hasidism in monolithic terms, is not averse to quoting non-Hasidic literature and is not too careful in providing exact sources. For our purpose, some of the material in Kasher is relevant but I have tried to be rather more exact in quoting the sources and providing dates as well as quoting from sources not found in Kasher.

According to the Hasidic master Mordecai of Lakhovich (1742–1810),[64] the individual in the Hereafter will be incapable of lust or evil desires but his bad character traits will remain part of his personality unless he had succeeded in eradicating them during his life on earth. And even in the soul of a great saint it is possible for there still to remain such traits as envy and pride. The first Hasidic author, R Jacob Joseph of Pulonnoye (d.*c.* 1782),[65] goes even further in seeing individuality as persisting in the Hereafter:

> I have heard that there is no Gehinnom in the future but they allow the wicked to enter Gan Eden and this in itself is their Gehinnom. For they

witness how the saints there pray and dance with joy and study the Torah assiduously and it is all a source of pain to them since they had never been familiar with such things. By those very things in which the saints delight the wicked are punished.

The nineteenth-century Hasidic master Jacob Leiner of Radzhyn comments,[66] in the name of his father, Mordecai Joseph of Izbica, on the Talmudic saying[67] that the saints in Paradise in relation to the Shekhinah will be like a candle in front of a flaming torch. The Talmud does not use the illustration of a candle burning during the day because the light of such a candle is not seen at all. The illustration of a candle and torch by night, on the other hand, suggests that the saints, while having some identity with the Shekhinah, will still preserve their own individuality. Their own light will shine even in the divine Presence. R Jacob Zevi of Parisov writes in similar vein[68] that while all souls stem from the same divine Source yet, once the soul has become separated from its Source in its sojourn on earth, it can never return to become totally absorbed in its Source: 'After the soul has departed this life, it returns on high, each soul in accordance to the stage it has reached through deeds performed in this world. Even a soul that has attained to the greatest elevation can never return to its Source in the Supernal One from Whom it had emanated.'

The Hasidic master and renowned preacher, R David Solomon Eibshütz (d. 1810), comments[69] on the Talmudic passage mentioned earlier that each saint is 'burnt'[70] by his neighbour's canopy, that a saint can comprehend on high only as much as his being can withstand. If a saint were to enter the 'canopy' of a saint with a higher degree of comprehension of the divine he would be 'burnt', i.e. he would lose his identity through the power of an illumination beyond his capacity to withstand. R Mordecai Joseph of Izbica (d. 1854),[71] on the other hand, interprets the Talmudic reference to the 'burning' to mean that, just as in this world each person has his own field of study, so, too, in the Hereafter each saint will be an expert, so to speak, in a particular degree of comprehension; each will outshine all the others in his special degree of comprehension as they will outshine him in theirs.

The idea appears frequently in Hasidic thought that, in this world, there is no permanent delight since once one has become familiar with a particular pleasure it leads to satiety and there is little delight any longer in the experience. All this is due to the limitations of bodily existence. Since the body is finite and limited, the ability of the soul to enjoy delight is restricted by its bodily habitation. But in the next world the soul has an existence beyond the constraints imposed by a physical body and so can enjoy the radiance of the Shekhinah permanently and without cessation. As R Jacob Joseph of Pulonnoye puts it:[72]

The difference between physical pleasure and the delight enjoyed by the soul is well known. Since the body is confined and restricted, any experience a person enjoys eventually becomes part of his natural capacity so that he enjoys the experience no longer. It is quite otherwise with regard to the delights enjoyed by the soul which, as a spiritual entity, has neither limits nor constraints. Such delight is infinite and unending and exists permanently.

R Shneor Zalman of Liady elaborates on the same idea:[73]

It is well known that the concept 'The World to Come' means that souls enjoy the radiance of the Shekhinah and this delight that the soul enjoys is nothing else but comprehension of the divine. For we know from experience that there is no enjoyment and no delight whatever unless the thing enjoyed has been grasped by the mind. It follows that delight in the divine must first become substantial and have a separate identity in the process of the soul's enjoyment before the soul can enjoy it.

Elsewhere[74] R Shneor Zalman writes that Gan Eden is formed from the precepts man carries out on earth. The performance of each good deed on earth draws down the radiance of the Shekhinah for the saints to enjoy in Gan Eden and this is 'a wondrous, infinite delight'.

The idea is also found in early Hasidic thought that the saints can enjoy the World to Come even while on earth. The early Hasidic master, Elimelech of Lizensk (1712–87), writes:[75]

A *tzaddik* who serves God by carrying out the *mitzvot* and keeps himself far from transgressing even the lightest commandment, and is meticulous in carrying out all his obligations in the best possible manner, yet has not attained to the stage in which his performance of the *mitzvot* brings him to attachment to the Creator, blessed be He, and to a great longing for Him, blessed be He; such a *tzaddik* has to wait for his recompense to be given to him in the World to Come. But there is a *tzaddik* who serves with great purity of thought and, through the *mitzvot*, attaches himself to the Creator, blessed be He, with great attachment and longing, seeing, at all times, how elevated the Creator is. Such a *tzaddik* does not need to wait in anticipation for the delights of the World to Come since he enjoys these same delights in this world.

If, as the above examples demonstrate, a movement with such a strong group emphasis as Hasidism can still depict Heavenly bliss in individualistic terms, it is hardly surprising that the intensely personal, highly individualistic Musar movement, founded by R Israel Lipkin of Salant, known as Israel Salanter (1810–83), should see it in these terms. The whole thrust of this Lithuanian movement, which has now won many adherents among non-Hasidic Jews, is to encourage individuals to strive for perfection. R Israel begins his famous *Iggeret ha-Musar*[76] ('Epistle of Musar') with the need for man to reflect, as a spur to virtuous living, on the fate of his soul in the Hereafter, though, unlike the Hasidic masters, he tends to dwell as much on the torments of Hell (conceived of, it should be said, in spiritual terms) as on the delights of Heaven:

Man is free in his imagination but bound by his reason. His imagination leads him wildly in the direction of his heart's desire, not fearing the inevitable future, when God will punish him for all his deeds, and he will be chastised by severe punishments, he alone, no other will be substituted. The sufferings of this world are small matters indeed, [comparing them] with the penalties for the sins. Man's soul abhors it [to such a degree] that a day will be considered a year.[77]

R Israel goes on to explain:[78]

Even without knowledge and understanding we do recognize the belief that permeates us that God is the Judge, to mete out to man his due, in accordance with his way of life. If his way of life is wicked and grievous he will be severely punished either in this world or in the World to Come, the everlasting world. Men do not realize to how great an extent [the punishment] will be meted out both as regards quality and quantity. However, if his deeds are pure and upright – he will be called blessed – [and he will be recompensed with] celestial pleasures in this [world] and even more so in the next [world], in a wonderful Eden, that is far beyond human intellect to comprehend.

It has been said that the difference between Hasidism and the Musar movement is that, while both believe that this world is nothing and the next world everything, Hasidism prefers to dwell on 'the next world is everything' while Musar tends to dwell on the 'this world is nothing'. But in both movements, when halting attempts are made to describe eternal bliss, the emphasis is more on the individual as individual than as member of the group.[79]

The latter-day Musar thinker, Rabbi E. E. Dessler (1891–1954), a great-grandson of Israel Salanter, is generally acknowledged as a foremost exponent of the Musar movement. Dessler's thought was also influenced by the Kabbalah and by Hasidism. As the spiritual mentor of the great Yeshivah of Ponievezh, in Bene Berak, Israel, Dessler influenced two generations of Orthodox students of the Torah and his writings still enjoy great popularity in Orthodox circles. Dessler's essay 'The World to Come'[80] affords a keen insight into the way the Musarists conceive of individuality in the Hereafter.

Dessler first postulates that life, rightly understood, consists of whatever aim to which an individual directs his strivings. Life is defined as that in which the self is engaged to the exclusion of all else, somewhat reminiscent of Tillich's 'ultimate concern'. Striving should not be seen as something extraneous to life but as life itself. It is the very substance of human life. it follows that if the self directs its strivings to what Dessler calls 'worldly vanities' that self is itself vain and insignificant. But if the self directs its strivings to spiritual, namely other-worldly, concerns, that self enjoys the life of the World to Come even here on earth. When the soul, after the death of the body, ascends to Heaven, it suffers, at first, acute shame because of its lowly state. This is true even of the greatest saints who lived a life of complete holiness since these, too, had entertained, at times, the possibility that there is an alternative to their holy path. Although they were never really tempted to forsake their way, the very fact that the possibility had presented itself to them is ample reason for their shame and embarrassment when their souls ascend on high. Filled by shame, the soul appreciates all the more God's kindness to such lowly creatures in bringing them nearer to Him. This greater awareness, in turn, causes the soul to appreciate to an even greater degree God's kindness and this leads to an increasing awareness of that kindness and so it proceeds *ad infinitum*. Thus the saint is not only in a state of increasing awareness of God's kindness in relation to his own unworthiness but, in the process, the soul constantly makes itself anew in ever-increasing degrees of comprehension of the divine. Moreover, it is only by the individual's free choice of the good, in his struggle with temptation in this life, that the good becomes part of his very being and his choosing of it the root of his eternal bliss in the World to Come. A good given as a gift, even if the gift is from God Himself, cannot become part of the soul's very being since a gift is an external endowment and is not self-acquired. This is why the Rabbis speak frequently of this life as a preparation for eternal life in the Hereafter.

Dessler continues:[81]

From this we learn how vast is the difference between one who is potentially good right from the beginning and one who freely makes the good his own. The man with potential for good from the beginning will always have that potential but this can never qualify as 'The World to Come' since it has been actualized neither in his comprehension nor in his own being. On the other hand, even the smallest fragment, if it has been acquired through effort, is in itself the life of the World to Come. Concerning this it is said (Proverbs 16:26): 'He that laboureth laboureth for himself.' We must, therefore, be exceedingly strong in withstanding temptation and to acquire in ourselves states of being produced by the Torah. For it is only through these that we shall see light and joy for ever for all eternity. Heaven forbid that we be satisfied with the virtues we already possess for it is not through these that we will attain to the great future. This is a principle from which we cannot depart: 'He that laboureth laboureth for himself.'

For all Dessler's indebtedness to Hasidic thought, as can be seen when his ideas are compared with those found in the selections from Hasidic writings given above, he, a loyal Musarist, does not ignore the doctrine of Gehinnom in his discussion of the fate of the individual in the next world.[82] But he is too sophisticated a religious thinker to see Hell as in anything but spiritual terms. Gehinnom, for Dessler, is the spiritual state of remoteness from God and the pain the soul suffers from such remoteness until it is purged of its evil. When the classical sources of Judaism describe the torments of Gehinnom in crudely physical terms, these are intended only as pointers to the spiritual torments the sinful soul will suffer. Dessler gives a cruel illustration of his own. The soul of the individual whose interests while on earth were in material things will be forced on itself in terrible boredom and isolation since material interests have obviously no place in the realm of the spirit.

In modern Jewish thought the swing is pronounced from the other-worldly to the this-worldly approach to Judaism, to the extent that the vocabulary of the Hasidic masters and the Musarists seems, for many modernists, vague, incomprehensible and irrelevant. Yet it cannot be ignored that, in the eighteenth century, the age of the beginnings of the Haskalah ('Enlightenment') movement, the pioneer of the Haskalah, Moses Mendelssohn (1729–86), wrote his *Phaedon*[83] with the express aim of defending the doctrine of immortality. Mendelssohn believed that the basic truths of religion such as belief in God and immortality are based not on revelation but on human reason and hence are not 'Jewish' specifically but universal; which is why he based his work on Plato's *Phaedon* and its hero, Socrates, is made to speak in the language of an 'enlightened' philosopher of the eighteenth century.

In the twentieth century, the Jewish existentialist thinker, Franz Rosenzweig (1886–1929), discusses immortality only perfunctorily in his *Star of Redemption*[84] as a very small part of his general philosophy of Judaism. The tone of the work is such as to give the impression not that Rosenzweig does not believe in immortality or that the belief is unimportant but that the main concern of the Jew should be with life in the here and now. And, like many moderns, Rosenzweig seems to be reluctant to explore the realm of the unknown. His lengthy and difficult book concludes with the words:

> To walk humbly with thy God – the words are written over the gate, the gate which leads out of the mysterious miraculous light of the divine sanctuary in which no man can remain alive. Whither, then, do the wings of the gate open? Thou knowest it not? INTO LIFE.

CHAPTER 12

Conclusion: A question of emphasis

Although the theme of this book, the significance of the individual in Judaism, is not irrelevant to the contemporary discussion among Jewish thinkers on the right of the individual to interpret Judaism in the light of his own knowledge and conscience, the two questions are different from one another. Individual autonomy within Judaism is not at all the same as individual significance according to Judaism. Even if, as I would argue, contemporary religious Jews ought to prefer that interpretation of Judaism which sees the individual as supremely important in the eyes of God, so to speak, it by no means follows that the ultimately significant individual is free to reject the Torah where his conscience tells him so to do. His ultimate significance may depend on total submission to the demands of the Torah whether or not he finds these congenial. Conversely, even if Judaism is interpreted as endowing the group with ultimate significance, it does not follow that the individual is debarred from exercising his conscience and following this wherever it leads. Nevertheless, the question of individual autonomy within Judaism cannot be ignored even in a book with the different aim of defending the ultimate significance of the individual.

On the question of individual autonomy, Eugene B. Borowitz[1] has argued precisely here is the divide between Orthodoxy and Liberal, Reform and Conservative versions of Judaism. According to Borowitz, the latter groups, in varying degrees, hold fast to their right to dissent from some aspects of the tradition. He rightly remarks that in Orthodoxy the Halakhah sets the limits of personal autonomy whereas in liberal versions, personal autonomy, though set in a frame of Jewish commitment, determines the effective bounds of Jewish 'law'. Since liberal Jews hold that the Torah, seen historically, is a human creation, it must follow that other human beings have their own right of dissent without such dissent being seen as a rejection of the divine will.[2] 'Liberals charge', says Borowitz,[3] 'that the Torah contains precepts which are unethical and hence are better understood as a product of early human spirituality rather than as God's perfect, eternal commands.' Borowitz's own view is to stress the covenantal aspects of Judaism according to which God and human beings are partners, with the corollary that conscientious dissent from what Jewish tradition once required or strongly urged is allowed and, on occasion, desirable.

It should not be thought, however, that all Orthodox thinkers have no room in their theology for the idea of personal autonomy. Borowitz acknowledges this. We might refer, especially, to two contemporary, Orthodox theologians, Sol Roth[4] and David Hartman,[5] who have given careful and original thought to the question.

In the chapter 'Human Rights',[6] Roth argues that human rights, in Judaism, follow on human obligations rather than the other way round. Secondly, the obligations are divinely prescribed, and thirdly the religiously minded individual believes that it is his duty to abide by them and, consequently, to respect the rights that these obligations imply.

Roth's attempt to analyse the connection between human rights and human obligations is keen but not entirely convincing, as when, for instance, he remarks:[7] 'I cannot authorize another to steal, even from me. I can present him with that which belongs to me as a gift, but I cannot allow him to take something from me by theft.' It is hard to see how, if I allow someone to steal from me, this can constitute 'theft'. But this is no doubt a mere quibble which should not be allowed to obscure Roth's significant contribution to the debate.

In his chapter on 'Freedom',[8] Roth contends that human rights are conditioned to some extent by the cultural context in which they are given expression so that, for example, freedom as an 'American' ideal (Roth, like many American Jewish thinkers, ignores in discussing Judaism the fact that there are adherents of Judaism living outside the USA) is different from freedom as a Jewish ideal. 'Freedom, in Jewish life, is a *national* goal; in the American perspective, it is an *individual* objective.' Consequently, according to Roth, who here seems to agree with Borowitz's view of Orthodoxy, the individual Jew is not granted the right to choose his beliefs; even the right to worship God as he sees fit. Nor is he permitted to deviate from Rabbinic injunctions. While acknowledging that Judaism tolerates, and even encourages, the expression of individual views on matters where the law is uncertain, Roth states that there remains, in the Jewish view, 'a large class of principles and precepts about which controversy was, to say the least, discouraged'.

So we come to Roth on 'Individualism'.[9] Roth argues: (1) that the individualism Judaism advocates is heroism in the fulfilment of *obligations* rather than in the exercise of *rights*; (2) it often assigns an importance to the individual as great as that which it associates with the community, because of the *value* inherent in personality; and (3) it encourages intellectual opposition, even while it insists on obedience, to authority.[10] The evidence adduced in this book demands the substitution in (2) of 'generally' or, at least, 'also' for 'often', and the precise meaning of (3) is far from clear. If Judaism encourages intellectual opposition to authority, why should it, at the same time, demand obedience to that authority. Roth tries valiantly to defend his contention that while Judaism does demand conformity in practice, it allows intellectual diversity and opposition, but the examples he adduces are from the Talmud whereas, as he himself says, in the other chapter quoted, Judaism, according to what Roth considers the Orthodox view, does not tolerate intellectual dissent even in theory. In short, for all his emphasis on the importance of the individual, Roth seems to have little appreciation that Judaism has had a history so that it is precarious, to say the least, to see Judaism as a static entity in relation to which the individual Jew can have no choice but to be either submissive or dismissive.

Of all the Orthodox theologians who have grappled with the problem none has adopted so radical a stance on autonomy as Hartman, so much so that his Orthodoxy has become suspect in some quarters. Hartman, like Borowitz, bases his view on the covenantal interpretation of Judaism. He argues[11] that in the Biblical and Rabbinic tradition there are two contrasting themes. One of these places the emphasis on the dignity of human responsibility and covenantal mutuality with God, whereas the other demands utter silence and resignation before the inscrutable transcendent will of God. Erich Fromm,[12] Hartman points out, strives to uncover the humanistic, non-authoritarian framework in the Judaic tradition to the extent that his inquiry results in a virtual obliteration of the other element, while Isaiah Leibowitz[13] tends towards the view that, at its highest level, Judaism inculcates an attitude of total submission to the will of God, in which the Jew carries out the *mitzvot* not because they are 'reasonable' or because they assist human strivings and human needs but because that is what it is that God commands. In J. B. Soloveitchik[14] Hartman detects an acceptance of both strands in the tradition, the submissive and the autonomous. In part critical of his mentor, Soloveitchik, Hartman follows a similar line of synthesis.

Hartman is chiefly concerned with the compatibility of individual freedom with the Halakhic tradition. He points, like Borowitz, to the inevitable tensions between submission to a fixed legal system and personal decisions in the organization of one's own life. He admits that the tradition has been interpreted so as virtually to deny individual initiative, except in the use of analogy in the application of the given law to new social and economic conditions. Yet, he claims, there is that other strand in the tradition itself which allows for far more critical reflection. Hartman writes:[15] 'I show that the tension between self-assertion and submission can be found in nearly all aspects of the rabbinic tradition. Terror and feelings of human insignificance before God appear together with a Promethean spirit in which halakhic teachers assert their intellectual strength and moral adequacy to define the directions of the covenant.'

It soon becomes clear, however, that when he speaks of individual autonomy Hartman means the autonomy of the individual Jew as a member of the covenantal community, so that what he is really talking about is not so much the individual versus the group or the community but rather the humanistic versus the God-is-all interpretation of Judaism. This is clear from Hartman's Postscript in which he seeks to go beyond his hero, Maimonides:[16]

> When Maimonides wrote, there was a sociocultural ambience that supported belief in miracle and divine reward and punishment. Theodicies that presupposed belief in the resurrection of the dead were then a reasonable way for making sense of human suffering. The fear of hell and anticipation of the joys of heaven were part of the way one experienced God's providential relationship to the *community* [italics mine]. This way of experiencing God is not a live and significant option for myself or many other modern Jews. It is not that I consider the *Treatise on Resurrection* false or childish or contrary to scientific enlightenment. Rather, it is not the way I experience Judaism as a living faith. It therefore would be inauthentic for me to articulate a philosophy of Judaism in the spirit of that treatise.

If this is individualism it is an individualism that is culturally conditioned. Such a view may or may not be acceptable to 'many modern Jews' but it has little to do with our theme of the significance of the individual in the Jewish tradition and is the direct antithesis of the traditional view described in the previous chapter of this book, a view which I share, that it is the ultimate fate of the individual for all eternity that is Judaism's chief concern, a view that does not necessarily imply that a modern Jew is obliged to swallow whole all the earlier speculations about Heaven and Hell and the resurrection.

In effect, all who write on the question of individual autonomy within the Jewish tradition agree that the individual cannot demand or be given complete autonomy if he is to remain within the tradition. It is an obvious absurdity to maintain that there can be a religious tradition in which the tradition as a whole is rejected by individual members of that tradition. So the question really comes down to where the parameters are drawn, to what the limits are when an individual's dissent is a voluntary stepping out from the tradition as a whole. On this, naturally, Jewish theologians will differ in accordance with their general philosophy of what Judaism teaches. In other words, the question of religious dissent, important though it is, is not really germane to the question of the role and significance of the individual in Judaism.

Another source of inquiry is the relation of general discussions of the individual and society to the question of the individual in a religious tradition. In the secular world the division between totalitarian regimes and democracies lies precisely in this area. R. B. Perry's analysis of 'The Individual as the Seat of Value'[17] takes us to the heart of this relationship. According to Perry, in a democratic individualism, the 'good life' is what the individuals in a society want, not as decided for them in paternalistic fashion by benefactors who may give in order to satisfy themselves rather than the recipients. 'The intent of the democratic state is to give people what *they* want instead of what the government wants for them.'[18] Perry also rightly points out that individualism is not egoism since the needs of the individual are to realize all his potential including his potential as a member of society. Nor is individualism anti-social. On the contrary, individualism can flourish only in an organized society. As Perry puts it,[19] individualism is 'the most exquisite and fragile flower of that historic human enterprise which is called civilization'.

Perry[20] traces the democratic insistence back to Christian teaching:

> In this insistence that the values by which institutions are justified reside in the individuals who live under them, democracy follows the main current

of the Christian tradition. The Gospel is a saving of souls – the souls of individual men and women. It stresses the love of persons, as the motive even of creation itself and as the highest form of human activity. Both protestantism and Catholicism, true to this tradition, have sharply condemned the totalitarian exaltation of the corporate state.

Fair enough. But all that Perry has to say about the Christian influence can and should be applied to Judaism, the source of the Christian attitude. As we have tried to demonstrate, any interpretation of Judaism which does not place the significance of the individual soul at its centre is misguided.

In this connection, however, a rider has to be added. Although, throughout this book, the term 'individual' has been used, the sober fact remains that, as noted in chapter 1, there is no word for 'individual' in classical Hebrew, not, at least, in the abstract sense in which the term is used by John Stuart Mill in his famous essay *On Liberty*.[21] Kathleen Nott[22] faults Mill on these very grounds, that it is difficult to see how the abstraction can be given concrete form. The same would apply to the term 'person', also an abstraction foreign to the thought of classical Judaism. Yet, though the note of caution is in order, the basic thesis of this book is not affected, provided it is realized that the whole discussion moves by means of translation from one culture to another.[23]

The religious question differs from the ethical question of the relationship between the individual and society, in that the religious person has a relationship with his God as well as with his fellows. In Kierkegaard's understanding of the *'Akedah* ('the Binding of Isaac', Genesis chapter 22), entitled *Fear and Trembling*,[24] the individual 'knight of faith' engages in a 'teleological suspension of the ethical'. Abraham goes in fear and trembling, uncertain whether his God really wants him to murder his son, but, as 'a knight of faith' whose ultimate relationship is with God, he is ready to carry out the fearful act if God demands it. Jewish thinkers have often argued that Judaism knows nothing of Kierkegaard's 'teleological suspension of the ethical' but, as I have tried to show elsewhere,[25] there are some Jewish sources on the *'Akedah* which come very close to the Kierkegaardian view, according to which the ultimate relationship of the religious individual is with his God and with no other.[26] But Kierkegaard is very one-sided in any event, as the critics of religious existentialism have not been slow to point out.[27]

The previous chapters of this book have examined the role of the individual, as Judaism sees it, in relation to himself, his family, his neighbour, the community and to God, and it has been argued that, in one sense, Judaism centres around the individual. In one sense but not, of course, in all. For it would not be at all difficult to present a very different picture of Judaism in which, to be sure, the importance of the individual is not ignored, but is made subservient to the Jewish people as a whole or even to humanity as a whole. In other words, it is simply not possible to treat Judaism in monolithic terms. The entity that we call Judaism is the product not alone of a divine revelation to passive human recipients but also of the reflections, adaptations, interpretations and dynamic re-interpretations of the revelation by Jews in many different lands living and working against the background of the various civilizations with which Jews became associated throughout the long history of the people. Any attempt at getting rid of what are supposed to be accretions in order to discover a 'normative Judaism' is bound to fail since the 'accretions' themselves are part of the totality.

It is simply not possible to give a neat answer to the question, for instance, whether Judaism is particularistic or universalistic or whether it is this-worldly or other-worldly or, in our case, whether the religion centres on the group or on the individual. Some Jews have tended to stress the universalistic aspects of Judaism, others its particularism. Some have seen Judaism in other-worldly terms, others in this-worldly, and, by the same token, some have seen Judaism as centring on the group, others as on the individual. To take any aspect of Judaism and to treat it as the norm by quoting proof-texts is to court failure since texts can easily be multiplied on the other side. Ultimately, it is not a question of either / or but of both this / and this, with the individual deciding where to place the emphasis; to choose to live by the emphasis which caters to his spiritual needs while acknowledging that a different emphasis is desirable for those with different needs. Indeed, the same individual may favour one emphasis at one time in his life and under particular circumstances and yet prefer a different emphasis in other times and circumstances. It is no mere quibble to affirm that this fact in itself demonstrates that the individual must be significant, since the final choice is his and his alone. There is no escaping individual responsibility. Even if the individual declares that he is willing to surrender to the tradition, that, too, is an individual choice and, on many of the most important issues, the tradition is itself many-sided.

Philo and Maimonides, granted their particular environment and the philosophy that emerged from it, felt themselves bound to place the emphasis on the doctrine of the immortality of the soul, while Nahmanides, against a different backcloth, felt himself bound to defend the doctrine of the resurrection.

What, then, does a book such as this seek to achieve in addition to purely scholarly investigation? The simple answer is that, when, for good and natural reasons, the contemporary thrust of Jewish thought is more in the direction of the group, it is perhaps useful to see the other side. If it should happen that, in some future time, the significance of the individual in Judaism would be so stretched as to endanger group loyalties, it would be necessary to redress the balance by pointing out that there can be no Judaism without the Jewish people.

Perhaps the Midrash (Exodus Rabbah 5:9) can have the last word:

Scripture says: 'The voice of the Lord is with power' (Psalm 29:4), not 'with *His* power' but *with power*, that is to say, according to the capacity of each individual, even to pregnant women according to their strength, thus to each person it was according to his strength. R Jose b. Hanina says, 'If you are doubtful of this, then think of the manna that descended with a taste varying according to the taste of each individual Israelite. The young men, eating it as bread; the old as wafers made with honey; to the babes it tasted like rich breast milk; to the sick, it was like fine flour mingled with honey; while to the heathen, its taste was bitter and like coriander seed. Now if the manna, which is all of one kind, became converted into so many kinds to suit the capacity of each individual, was it not even more possible for the Voice, which had power, to vary according to the capacity of each individual that no harm should come to him?'

Glossary

Adam Kadmon 'Primordial Man', the Kabbalistic name for the stage in the unfolding of the *Sefirot* at which these are still undifferentiated and exist only in potential.

Aggadah 'Telling', the non-legal parts of the Talmud.

Aggadot Plur. of 'Aggadah'; Talmudic legends, tales and homilies.

Aḥad ha-'Am 'One of the people', pen-name of Asher Ginsberg (1856–1927).

'Akedah 'Binding' of Isaac, Genesis, chapter 22.

'Amidah 'Standing' Prayer, the prayer recited thrice daily in a standing position.

Amora 'Speaker' or 'expounder', the name given to the teachers (plur. Amoraim) in Babylon and Palestine whose views are stated throughout the Palestinian and Babylonian Talmuds. The main thrust of their debates and discussion revolves around the Mishnah, hence they are the 'expounders' of the Mishnah and the words of the Tannaim generally.

Avot 'Fathers', the name of a tractate of the Mishnah, popularly known in English as 'Ethics of the Fathers' or 'Sayings of the Fathers'.

Bet Yosef 'House of Joseph', title of the Commentary to the *Tur* by R Joseph Karo (sixteenth century).

dat 'Law', a Persian loan-word in the Talmud for 'law' and, in the middle ages, for 'religion'.

En Sof 'Without Limit', the Kabbalistic name for the Infinite Ground of Being, God as He is in Himself, in contradistinction to God as manifested in the *Sefirot*.

Gaon 'Excellency', plur. Geonim. The title of the post-Talmudic heads of the Academies in Babylon down to the end of the tenth century.

Gemara 'Teaching', a synonym for 'Talmud'.

Ḥabad From the initial letters of *Ḥokhmah* ('Wisdom'), *Binah* ('Understanding'), *Da'at* ('Knowledge'); the name of the intellectual, contemplative sect within Hasidism founded by R Shneor Zalman of Liady, now also known as Lubavitch, after the Russian town of that name which was the home of Shneor Zalman's son and successor.

Halakhah 'Walking' in God's ways. The legal parts of the Talmud (in contradistinction to the Aggadah); also used for Jewish law in general.

Hanukkah 'Dedication', the winter feast of lights during which candles are lit in a special ceremony.

ḥasid 'Pietist', plur. *ḥasidim*, the name given to adherents of Hasidism.

Hasidism The mystical, pietistic movement founded by Israel Baal Shem Tov (1698–1760).

Havdalah 'Division', the ceremony at the termination of the Sabbath when benedictions are recited over wine, light and spices to mark the distinction between the Sabbath and the weekdays.

ḥerem The ban pronounced by the court on certain classes of offenders.

Kabbalah 'Tradition', the mystical, theosophical system developed in the twelfth century in Provence and later in other centres.

Khazars A kingdom in Eastern Europe during the seventh and tenth centuries the king and subjects of which, at one time, embraced Judaism. Judah Halevi (d. 1141) wrote his defence of Judaism, the *Khuzari*, in the form of a dialogue between the Khazar king and a Rabbi.

Maskil 'Enlightened', a follower of the eighteenth-century Enlightenment Movement which sought to accommodate Jewish life to Western society.

Midrash The process of Scriptural exegesis in homiletical fashion; plur. Midrashim, the name for various collections of these, such as Midrash Rabbah, 'The Great Midrash'.

minyan 'Number', the quorum of ten required before some of the sacred, public prayers can be recited.

Mishnah 'Teaching', the name for the digest of Judaism compiled by Rabbi Judah the Prince in Palestine around the year 220 CE.

Mitnaggedim 'Protestants', the Rabbinic and communal leaders who opposed the spread of Hasidism in their belief that the movement was subversive.

Noahide laws The seven rules of natural law and religion, obedience to which is demanded of Gentiles (the sons of Noah) as well as of Jews.

'Olam ha-Ba 'World to Come', the Hereafter, the next world.

peot 'Corners' of the head, to be left unshaven by pious Jews.

Purim The festival recorded in the book of Esther in celebration of the deliverance of the Jews from Haman's plot to destroy them.

Rosh ha-Shanah 'Beginning of the year', the Jewish New Year festival on which the *shofar*, 'ram's horn', is sounded.

Seder 'Order', the festive meal partaken of on the first night of Passover in celebration of the Exodus.

Sefirot 'Numbers', the ten powers or potencies of the Godhead in manifestation, in contradistinction to *En Sof*.

sevara 'Theory', common sense or sound argument.

Shavuot The Feast of Weeks, Pentecost.

sheḥitah The correct manner of killing an animal for food.

Shekhinah 'Divine Presence', often personified as a female.

Shema '*Hear*' O Israel', the Jewish declaration of faith recited twice daily (Deuteronomy 6:4).

Shulḥan 'Arukh 'Arranged Table', the standard Code of Jewish Law compiled in the sixteenth century by R Joseph Karo with glosses by R Moshe Isserles, the latter known as the *Rema*, after the initial letters of his name.

Simḥat Torah 'Rejoicing of the Law', the joyous celebration of the Torah at the end of the Festival of Tabernacles.

sugya 'Layout', a complete unit of the Talmud, a Talmudic passage in its entirety.

sukkah 'Booth', the tent-like structure in which devout Jews have their meals on Tabernacles.

tallit 'Robe', the prayer shawl with fringes (Numbers 15:37–41) worn by men during the daytime prayers.

Talmud The teachings of the Amoraim as recorded in Palestine (around the year 400 CE) and in Babylon (around the year 500 CE). The former constitutes the Palestinian Talmud (or the Jerusalem Talmud), the latter the Babylonian Talmud. The name refers to the Babylonian Talmud unless the other is specified.

Tanna 'Teacher', plur. Tannaim. The teachers in Palestine of the first two centuries CE whose doctrines are found in the Mishnah and in works contemporaneous with the Mishnah.

Tefillah 'Prayer', the statutory prayer.

tefillin 'Phylacteries'.

Tikkuney Zohar A work belonging to the Zoharic corpus of literature.

Tisha be-Av 'Ninth of Av', the fast in commemoration of the destruction of the Temple, which is held on the ninth day of the month of Av.

Torah 'Doctrine' or 'teaching', originally the name for the Pentateuch but extended to embrace Judaism as a whole.

Tosafists The name for the mediaeval glossators whose arguments are printed together with the text in most editions of the Babylonian Talmud.

Tur 'Row', also known, in the fuller form, as *Turim*; the name of the Code of law, compiled, in four great sections or 'rows', by R Jacob b. Asher (d. 1340).

tzibbur 'Community'.

Zaddik 'Saint', leader of group and its mentor in Hasidism.

Zohar 'Illumination' or 'Splendour', the mystical Commentary to the Pentateuch compiled in Spain at the end of the thirteenth century.

Notes

1 INDIVIDUAL SIGNIFICANCE

1 It is astonishing that in neither the old *Jewish Encyclopedia* nor in the *Encyclopedia Judaica* is there an article on the role of the individual in Judaism. The *Universal Jewish Encyclopedia* does have an article entitled 'Individualism' (by Samuel J. B. Wolk, vol. v, pp. 559–63) but this article deals with individualism as a philosophy of free thought and has hardly anything to say about our theme. The short article 'Individuality' by Peter Ochs in *Contemporary Jewish Religious Thought*, ed. Arthur A. Cohen and Paul Mendes-Flohr, New York, 1987, pp. 483–5, similarly contains little of relevance.

2 See, e.g., H. Maldwyn Hughes, *The Ethics of Jewish Apocryphal Literature*, London, n.d., p. 245: 'In the OT, up to the time of Jeremiah, moral responsibility is attached to the nation, and not to the individual, and consequently the sanctions to which appeal is made are national rather than individual. Solidarity, not individualism, was the governing principle of pre-Exilic thought.' Against this notion see the salutory reminder by G. W. Anderson (*The Old Testament and Modern Study*, ed. H. H. Rowley, Oxford, 1956, p. 309): 'The untenability of the older view that "individualism emerged" in the seventh century or later is but one example of the inadequacy of neat patterns for describing the development of Israel's religion.'

3 It should be noted that in the Joseph saga, for instance, the background of rivalry between the tribes of Judah and Ephraim is overlaid with a narrative about individuals in conflict.

4 Cf. the Adam and Eve and Noah narratives, where, although obviously with the background idea of humanity as a whole, the stories are told as about individuals.

5 It is not denied that the singular is sometimes used for laws directed to the people, e.g. in Deuteronomy 20, but in these instances the context makes it clear that the concern is with the people, i.e. because of the social and political considerations. On the 'I' of the Psalms, whether individual or communal, see A. R. Johnson in Rowley (ed.), *The Old Testament and Modern Study*, pp. 202f.

6 This is not to ignore the notorious difficulties in the enterprise, occasioned chiefly by the large amount of purely legendary material.
7 *Shabbat* 31a.
8 *Berakhot* 16b–17a.
9 See *ET*, vol. III, under *ben noaḥ*, pp. 348ff.
10 *Sifra*, ed. I. H. Weiss, p. 86b; *Bava Kama* 38a.
11 *Yalkut* to Judges 4:4, from *Tanna de-Ve Eliyahu*.
12 See I. Husik, *A History of Mediaeval Jewish Philosophy*, New York, 1958, for the views of the mediaeval Jewish philosophers.
13 See my *Principles of the Jewish Faith*, 2nd edn, Northvale and London, 1988, for an extensive bibliography on Maimonides' views.
14 Maimonides' analysis of the 'reasons for the precepts' in the third section of his *Guide* is almost entirely on the grounds of individual self-perfection.
15 See the articles on the Lurianic Kabbalah in *Jewish Spirituality*, ed. Arthur Green, vol. II, New York, 1987, pp. 7ff.
16 See G. Scholem, *The Messianic Idea in Judaism*, New York, 1971, pp. 176ff. It might here be remarked that the whole thrust of the non-Hasidic Lithuanian Musar Movement, founded by Israel Salanter, is in the direction of individual self-perfection (see pp. 109–11).
17 *Berakhot* 58a.
18 See note of Z. H. Chajes (in Romm edn, Vilna), who quotes other Rabbinic sources (e.g. Midrash Numbers Rabbah 21:15) in which there is no reference specifically to Israel. Chajes observes that this fits in better with the reason given, that their faces and minds are different.
19 *Avot* 6:1.
20 *Berakhot* 17b; *Ta'anit* 24b.
21 *Shabbat* 30b.
22 See *Aḥad ha-'Am*, Collected Works, *'Al Parashat Derakhim*, Berlin, 1921, vol. II, pp. 66–79; English trans., *Essays, Letters, Memoirs – Ahad ha-Am*, by Leon Simon, Oxford, 1946, 'Judaism and Nietzsche', pp. 76–82.
23 In Walter Kaufmann (ed.) *Religion from Tolstoy to Camus*, New York, 1961, pp. 436–7.
24 Søren Kierkegaard, *The Last Years Journals 1853–55*, ed. and trans. Ronald Gregor Smith, London, 1965, p. 146.
25 Quoted by Robert G. Olson, *An Introduction to Existentialism*, New York, 1963, p. 166. See the whole of chapter 6, 'The Other', in Olson, pp. 162–91.
26 For the views of Heidegger on this theme see David E. Roberts, *Existentialism and Religious Belief*, New York, 1959, pp. 149–64.
27 *be-Malkhut ha-Yahadut*, Jerusalem, 1959. For Sevin's story see p. 13.

2 SELF-REALIZATION AS A RELIGIOUS VALUE

1 The two sayings of R Simhah Bunem have often been quoted, e.g. in Martin Buber: *Tales of the Hasidim*, New York, 1947–8, vol. II, pp. 249–50 and 256.

2 See Mishnah *Yoma* 8:9 and cf. Maimonides, *Yad*, *Berakhot* 11:2, *Kesef Mishneh*. Maimonides uses the expression '*Mitzvot* between man and his neighbour' referring to the positive precepts such as alms-giving and acts of kindness. Further investigation is required, but I have been unable to discover in the Rabbinic literature the expression 'between man and his neighbour' as applied to positive precepts, only with regard to negative precepts, ' '*averot* between man and his neighbour', as in the Mishnah in *Yoma*. It is possible that, for the Talmudic Rabbis, while it is possible to make a distinction between *offences* against God and against the neighbour, no distinction is made with regard to positive precepts, *mitzvot*, since a *mitzvah* is a positive command to do this or that, the divine Commander being the same whether He commands 'religious' or 'ethical' acts. Even in the latter instance, it is not the neighbour's commands that are being obeyed. In connection with offences, on the other hand, it is possible to distinguish between acts which offend only God and acts which offend the neighbour as well.

3 There is, of course, an obligation for a man to care for his physical well-being and *a fortiori* for his advance in spirituality but, in the Rabbinic literature, both of these belong in the category 'between man and God', i.e. the aim is the direct service of God. It should be noted that the saying (*Genesis Rabbah* 44, ed. J. Theodor and H. Albeck, pp. 424–5), 'The *mitzvot* were given to refine [*le-tzaref*] people' refers to *all* the *mitzvot* (the illustration given is of the command to kill animals for food in the special manner of *sheḥitah*) and is not relevant to the question of the division of *mitzvot* into categories.

4 Book III, chapter 25, ed. I. Husik, Philadelphia, 1944, vol. III, pp. 217f.

5 See Husik's note on p. 218 for the source in Aquinas, *Summa*, *Prima*, *Secunda*, XCIX: *moralia*, *caeremonialia* and *indicialia*.

6 Cf. the concluding chapter of Albo's Book III for the development of this idea.

7 *Bava Kama* 30a; *Maharsha* in Romm edn, Vilna, of the Talmud to the passage.

8 *Kiddushin* 40a.

9 *Shelah*, Amsterdam, 653; Jerusalem, 1963, *sha'ar ha-otiot*, 4, pp. 45b–47a.

10 The early Maskil, Pinhas Elijah Horowitz of Vilna (d. 1821) refers to our theme in a humanistic way in his *Sefer ha-Berit*, Part II, *maamar* 13, chapter 25, Warsaw, 1881, pp. 330–1. This author speaks of three duties or obligations (*ḥovot*): man's obligations to God, to himself and to his fellows. Horowitz, claiming to be the first Jewish author to note this in detail, is at pains to point out that the category of obligation to the neighbour applies to non-Jews as well as to Jews (see his remarks here and, especially, at the beginning of this *maamar*, pp. 308f). Horowitz remarks ironically that everyone carries out the obligations to the self and very many the obligations to God but the obligations a man has to his fellows are often overlooked. Another nineteenth-century author in similar vein is Israel Lipschitz who, in his Commentary to the Mishnah, *Tiferet Yisrael*, to *Avot* 2:1, tries, somewhat artifically, to read the idea

into the Mishnah. According to Lipschitz, there are three categories (he adds the German form of each): (1) duties (*Pflichten*); (2) virtues (*Tugenden*); (3) good manners (*Sitten*).

11 See the informative but one-sided remarks of J. Epstein, *Mitzvot ha-Bayit*, New York, 1972, vol. I, Introduction, pp. 30–4. In Hasidic thought the highest form of self-realization, in the sense of penetration to the true, inner Self, the divine spark in man, is called *bittul ha-yesh*, 'annihilation of selfhood' (see the fuller treatment on pp. 55–6).

3 ATTITUDES TO LIFE AND DEATH

1 The popular saying that a suicide has no share in the World to Come, which would cause a far more severe punishment to be visited on the suicide than on one guilty of murder, has no support in any of the classical sources and receives no mention in the laws about suicide in the *Shulḥan 'Arukh, Yoreh De'ah* 345; see Responsa of Eliezer Fleckeles of Prague (1754–1826), *Teshuvah me-Ahavah*, Prague 1809–1821, no. 345. The Hebrew term for suicide is *meabbed 'atzmo la-da'at*, 'one who intentionally destroys himself'. Although the *Shulḥan 'Arukh* rules that the rites of mourning are not to be observed for a suicide, it is generally accepted that prayers for the repose of his soul are permissible and have merit; see the Responsa of Yosef Hayyim of Baghdad (d. 1909), *Rav Pe'alim*, Jerusalem, 1901–12, vol. III, *Yoreh De'ah* no. 30.

2 *Bava Kama* 91b. In the article on 'Suicide', *EJ* vol. 15, pp. 489–91, the statement (p. 489) that 'it [suicide] is nowhere explicitly forbidden *in the Talmud*' (italics mine) is incorrect. Possibly this is a misprint for 'in the Bible' or 'in the Torah'.

3 *Yad, Rotzeaḥ* 2:2–3.

4 See *Keli Ḥemdah* by Meir Dan Plotzki, Pietrikow, 1927, on *noaḥ* 3, on the verse in Genesis (9:5), vol. I, pp. 8b–10a, who expresses astonishment at Maimonides' statement that there is no 'death at the hands of the Court' for the crime of suicide. How could there be, since the one who committed the crime is no longer alive? Possibly Maimonides formulates it in this way to point out that suicide is a separate and lesser crime than murder.

5 *Ḥullin* 10a.

6 *Yad, Rotzeaḥ* 11:5.

7 *Nedarim* 40a.

8 *Ketubot* 104a. Cf. the story of R Joshua and the old woman tired of her life in *Yalkut, Mishley*, par. 943.

9 Responsa *Ḥikkekey Lev*, Salonika, 1840, vol. I, no. 40. The Boyaner Rebbe, R Moshe Friedmann, Responsa *Da'at Moshe*, Jerusalem, 1984, no. 15, p. 23, raises an objection to the *Ran* from *Berakhot* 10a: 'Let a man not despair of divine mercy even if a sharp sword rests on his neck.' But there the man wants to live whereas the *Ran* deals with the case of the man who has no wish to live. R Y. M. Epstein, in his *'Arukh ha-*

Shulḥan, Pietrikow, 1905, *Yoreh, De'ah* 335:3, rules in accordance with the *Ran*'s opinion.

10 Responsa *Tzitz Eliezer*, vol. v (Jerusalem, 1957), *Ramat Raḥel*, chapter 5, and vol. vii (Jerusalem, 1983), no. 49.

11 Vol. i, Vienna, 1860; Brooklyn, 1973, p. 61a. The question whether a man is allowed to curse himself (see H. H. Medini, *Sedey Ḥemed*, ed. A. I. Friedmann, New York, 1962, vol. i, pp. 166–7) is not strictly germane to our question since there it might be due to anger with the self and not to a wish of the self to be rid of its torments.

12 On this Hasidic thinker's religious determinism see J. G. Weiss, 'The Religious Determinism of Joseph Mordecai [sic] of Izbica' (Heb.), in S. Ettinger *et al.*, *Baer Jubilee Volume*, Jerusalem, 1960, pp. 447–53, and see above p. 106.

13 Lublin, 1922; Brooklyn and New York, 1973, pp. 72–3.

14 See, e.g., A. Markus, *ha-Ḥasidut*, Hebrew trans. by M. Shenfield, Tel-Aviv, 1954, p. 244.

4 FAMILY RELATIONSHIPS

1 Maimonides, *Yad*, *Evel* 2:1; *Shulḥan 'Arukh*, *Yoreh De'ah* 374:4.

2 *Yad*, *Evel* 13:12.

3 *Shulḥan 'Arukh*, *Yoreh De'ah* 251:3.

4 *Shulḥan 'Arukh*, *Yoreh De'ah* 240:14.

5 *Shulḥan 'Arukh*, *Yoreh De'ah* 240:21.

6 *Shulḥan 'Arukh*, *Yoreh De'ah* 240:22.

7 *Shulḥan 'Arukh*, *Yoreh De'ah* 240:24.

8 *Shulḥan 'Arukh*, *Yoreh De'ah* 240:24, in *Rema*.

9 *Yoreh De'ah* 240:25.

10 Responsa *Maharik*, Warsaw, 1884, no. 166. On the general question of parental authority and its limits see the study by Gerald Blidstein, *Honor Thy Father and Thy Mother*, New York, 1975.

11 *Kiddushin* 32a.

12 Tosafists to the passage, see under *oru*.

13 *Kiddushin* 31b.

14 Responsa *Minḥat Eleazar*, Munkacs, 1930, vol. iii, *Yoreh De'ah*, no. 6.

15 See D. Z. Hillmann, *Iggerot ha-Rav Ba'al ha-Tanya*, Jerusalem, 1953, pp. 142–4, for the Avigdor document in full.

16 See Hillmann, *Iggerot* for the details.

17 See Martin Buber, *Tales of the Hasidim*, New York, 1947–8, vol. ii, p. 57.

18 *No'am Elimelekh*, ed. G. Nigal, Jerusalem, 1978, to Genesis 12:1, vol. i, pp. 23–4.

19 Dov Baer of Meserich, *Or Torah*, Brooklyn, 1969, section *yitro*, pp. 67–8.

20 *Yevamot* 63b.

21 *Even ha-'Ezer* 1:4.

22 Commentary *Ha'amek Davar*. New York, 1972, to the Genesis verse, in note *harḥev davar*, p. 11a, note 1.

5 LOVING THE NEIGHBOUR

1 For this analysis of the plain meaning of Leviticus 19:18 see the remarks of E. Ullendorff, 'Thought Categories in the Hebrew Bible', in *Studies in Rationalism, Judaism and Universalism in Memory of Leon Roth*, ed. Raphael Loewe, London, 1966, pp. 276–8, to which I am indebted here.
2 *Yad, De'ah* 6:3.
3 Based on Jerusalem Talmud *Ḥagigah* 2:1 (77c).
4 *Gittin* 61a.
5 See, e.g., the note of J. H. Hertz in his *Pentateuch and Haftorahs*, London, 1960, pp. 563–4. It has been suggested that from the Tosafists to *Bava Kama* 38a, see under *'amad*, it can be inferred that these mediaeval teachers also hold that 'thy neighbour' in the verse is of unlimited application; see the commentaries of R Samuel Eliezer Edels (the *Maharsha*) and R Meir of Lublin (the *Maharam*) to the passage in *Bava Kama* and see above chapter 2, note 10, p. 127 on the view of Pinhas Elijah Horowitz in his *Sefer ha-Berit*.
6 See, e.g., Moses Cordovero's *Tomer Devorah*, Jerusalem, 1975, chapter 1, p. 5; in my translation, *The Palm Tree of Deborah*, London, 1960, pp. 52–3.
7 *Bava Metzia'* 2:11.
8 *Bava Metzia'* 33a.
9 *Avot* 5:10.
10 *Pesaḥim* 25b.
11 *Sanhedrin* 72a.
12 *Essays, Letters, Memoirs – Ahad ha-Am*, trans. Leon Simon, Oxford, 1946, pp. 128f.
13 In my book, *Jewish Values*, London, 1960, pp. 124–34, reproduced in *Contemporary Jewish Ethics*, ed. M. M. Kellner, New York, 1978, pp. 175–86.
14 *Bava Metzia'* 62a.
15 John 15:13.
16 On suicide as a different offence from murder see above p. 15.

6 COMMUNAL OBLIGATIONS

1 See S. W. Baron, *The Jewish Community*, Philadelphia, 1945, and my article, 'Judaism and Membership', in J. Kent and R. Murray (eds.), *Intercommunion and Church Membership*, London, 1973, pp. 141–53.
2 On the *ḥerem* and other methods of coercion in the Jewish community see D. M. Shohet, *The Jewish Court in the Middle Ages*, New York, 1931, chapter 7, pp. 133–50; article 'Ḥerem' in *EJ*, vol. VIII, pp. 344–55.
3 On the degree to which democratic procedures were followed in the ancient and mediaeval Jewish communities see Baron, *Jewish Community*, index 'Democracy'.
4 On the subject of women's rights in modern Judaism there is now a vast

literature. Here we need only refer to Susannah Heschel (ed.), *On Being a Jewish Feminist*, New York, 1983; and, for the historical background, Judith Romney Wegner, *Chattel or Person*, New York, 1988.

5 *Sanhedrin* 44a.
6 See the acute analysis by J. Katz, 'Though he Sinned, he Remains an Iṣraelite' (Heb.), in *Tarbitz*, 27 (1958), pp. 203–17.
7 The remark is attributed to George Steiner in Stephen Brook, *The Club*, London, 1989, p. 11.
8 See *Yevamot* 47a on the proselyte who returns to his pagan ways after his conversion to Judaism.
9 Some Orthodox Rabbis hold that a daughter, too, may recite the Kaddish (see, e.g., Jair Hayyim Bacharach, Responsa *Ḥavvot Yair*, Frankfurt, 1699, no. 222).
10 E.g. the mystic brotherhood in Safed. See S. Schechter's study of this brotherhood in his *Studies in Judaism*, Philadelphia, 1945, 2nd Series, pp. 202ff.
11 *Avot* 2:2.
12 R Travers Herford, *Sayings of the Fathers*, New York, 1962, p. 42.
13 *Avot* 2:4.
14 *Sayings of the Fathers*, p. 45.
15 *Avot* 2:3.
16 *Avot* 4:11.
17 *Avot* 5:18.
18 *Ta'anit* 11a; Henry Malter, *The Treatise Ta'anit of the Babylonian Talmud*, Philadelphia, 1928, p. 74.
19 *Ta'anit* 11a; Malter, *Ta'anit*, pp. 74–5.
20 *Rosh ha-Shanah* 17a.
21 *Bava Batra* 60b.
22 *Bava Kama* 79b. Cf. *'Avodah Zarah* 36a.
23 The *locus classicus* for communal taxation and voluntary contributions is *Bava Batra* 7b–11a.
24 Donations of money and goods for the upkeep of the Temple are known as *bedek ha-bayit*, 'the repair of the house'; free-will offerings for the altar are known as *nedarim*, 'vows', and *nedavot*, 'gifts'. Each individual was also expected to contribute to the perpetual offering, the *tamid*, known as a *korban tzibbur*, 'a communal offering'. Of relevance to our theme is the statement in the Talmud, *Menaḥot* 65a, that the Sadducees held that an individual could offer to defray the cost of the perpetual offering but the Pharisees held that the offering had to be from the Temple funds to which the people as a whole contributed.
25 *The Authorised Daily Prayer Book*, ed. Simeon Singer, London, 1962, p. 203.
26 Responsa *Rashba*, Lemberg, 1811, no. 581.
27 *Bava Batra* 133b.
28 *Yoreh De'ah* 249:13.
29 See the standard commentaries to the *Shulḥan 'Arukh* for whether Isserles rules as he does because otherwise the gift may later be sold by the

congregation (in which case where there exists an express stipulation that it cannot be sold the name should not be recorded) or whether it is because of 'remembrance' and is approved of by Isserles in all circumstances. Since Isserles has the *Rashba* as his source, the latter view seems to be the correct one.

30 For the details and on the general history of alms-giving and poor relief in Judaism see J. Bergmann, *ha-Tzedakah be-Yisrael*, Jerusalem, 1975. Zevi Elimelech Teicher's *Ma'aseh ha-Tzedakah*, Premisla, 1874, photocopy, Jerusalem, 1978, is a useful anthology of teachings on the high value of charity to the poor.

31 See Tosafists, *Ta'anit*, under *'aser te'aser*, and Isserles, *Shulḥan 'Arukh, Yoreh De'ah* 249:1, and see A. M. Albert, *Ma'aser Kesafim*, Jerusalem, 1977, for the various views on this subject.

32 *Ketubot* 50a.

33 Isserles in *Shulḥan 'Arukh, Yoreh De'ah* 249:1.

34 Shneor Zalman of Liady, 'Iggeret ha-Kodesh', in *Tanya*, Vilna, 1930, nos. 9–11.

35 *Mishneh Torah, Mattenot 'Aniyim* 10: 7–14.

36 See M. Greenberg, *Biblical Prose Prayers*, Berkeley, Calif., 1983.

37 A good deal of material on this subject from traditional sources is to be found in I. J. Fuchs, *ha-Tefillah be-Tzibbur*, Jerusalem, 1978.

38 *Bet ha-Beḥirah, Berakhot*, ed. S. Dickmann, Jerusalem, 1965, p. 15.

39 *Berakhot* 6a.

40 *Berakhot* 8a. Cf. *Berakhot* 29b–30a that even such an individual prayer as the wayfarer's prayer (*tefillat ha-derekh*) should be worded in the plural, not 'lead *me* to my destination' but 'lead *us* to our destination'.

41 E.g. the Kaddish and the Kedushah. – see *Berakhot* 21b and Palestinian Talmud, *Berakhot* 7:3 (11c).

42 See Fuchs, *ha-Tefillah*, pp. 38–44, for other views.

43 *Mishneh Torah, Tefillah* 8:1.

44 Zohar I, 234b; Fuchs, *ha-Tefillah*, p. 39.

45 *Ruaḥ Ḥayyim*, Vilna, 1859, Comment on *Avot* 2:13, p. 17a; *ha-Tefillah*, Fuchs, p. 40.

46 *Kuzari*, III:19: Fuchs, *ha-Tefillah*, pp. 40–1.

47 *Keritut* 6b.

48 Quoted by Fuchs, *ha-Tefillah*, p. 42.

49 See, e.g., *Makkot* 10a that scholars who study on their own become foolish and deserve that a sword should fall upon their neck and the saying of Rabbi quoted there: 'Much Torah have I learnt from my teachers, more from my colleagues and most of all from my disciples.'

50 See the famous account of the Oven of Akhnai in *Bava Metzia'* 69a–b where Rabbi Eliezer refuses to withdraw his opinion and is supported by a Heavenly voice and yet his colleagues still hold fast to their opinion and their opinion is accepted as the law; *'Eruvin* 13b; *Ḥullin* 11a.

51 See *Kiddushin* 30b on scholars becoming 'enemies'.

52 *Kiddushin* 32a–b.

53 *'Avodah Zarah* 19a.

54 For a similar suggestion that there is a difference between learning from books as we do nowadays and the older learning from the teacher, see H. M. Medini, *Sedey Ḥemed*, ed. A. I. Friedmann, New York, 1962, vol. III, p. 402, no. 145.
55 *Sanhedrin* 46a.
56 See *ET*, vol. II, under *apikoros*, pp. 136–7.

7 GOD AND THE SOUL

1 See David Baumgardt, *Great Western Mystics*, New York, 1961, p. 34 and p. 81 note 74. The references, given by Baumgardt, are: to Jerome, Commentary to Ezekiel, *liber* 1, *vers* 6, 7; to St Bernard, *Opera* (1781), *tom.* IV, p. 521b, *In Cantica Canticorum, serma* 18, 6; to St Bonaventura's *Opera omnia*, Quaracchi, vol. V (1891), *Itinerarium mentis in Deum*, chapters 11 and 13.
2 See Evelyn Underhill, *Mysticism*, London, 1940, p. 304.
3 See Baumgardt, *Western Mystics*, p. 82 note 78, where a full list is given of the sources in Eckhart.
4 Baumgardt, *Western Mystics*, p. 34 and p. 83 note 79. Cf. Jeanne Ancelot-Hustache *Master Ekhart*, in the 'Men of Wisdom' Series, London, 1957, trans. Hilda Graef, who says, 'He (Eckhart) also calls it "the ground" (*der grundt*); the "little castle" (*bürgelin*), above all "the spark of the soul" (*scinctilla animae, das fünkelin der sele*), an expression that comes from Peter Lombard, who borrowed it from St Jerome; but it has so often been cited with reference to Eckhart that it has almost become his special property' (pp. 65–6).
5 The *Chandogya Upanishad* (III, 14), quoted by George Foot Moore, *History of Religions*, Edinburgh, 1914, vol. I, pp. 273f.
6 C. Hartshorne and William L. Reese (eds.), *Philosophers Speak of God*, Chicago, Ill., 1953, p. 171, from *The Sacred Books of the East*, ed. Max Müller, Oxford, 1890, vol. XXXIV, pp. 14–15, 185–6. Cf. chapter 7 VII. Cf. 'Some Hindu Approaches', in R. C. Zaehner's *Mysticism Sacred and Profane*, Oxford, 1957, pp. 129–52. Aldous Huxley in his *The Perennial Philosophy*, London, 1958, chapter 1, pp. 14–35, gives some interesting illustrations from mystical writers on this theme throughout the ages, though it is doubtful, to say the least, if his interpretation of Hillel's famous saying, quoted on p. 28, is correct. A useful translation of the Upanishads dealing with the theme is *The Upanishads*, trans. Swami Prabhavananda and Frederick Manchester, New York, 1957. However, Rudolph Otto's comparative study of Sankara and Eckhart in his *Mysticism East and West*, trans. Bertha L. Bracey and Richenda C. Payne, New York, 1957, reminds us that not all mystical statements regarding the *scinctilla animae* and its identification with the Ground of Being mean the same thing.
7 See R. A. Nicholson, *The Mystics of Islam*, London, 1914, chapter 4, pp. 102–19, and chapter 6, pp. 148–68.
8 Nicholson, *Mystics of Islam*, p. 119.

9 *A Social and Religious History of the Jews*, 2nd edn, vol. VIII, New York, 1958, pp. 112–13.
10 R. C. Zaehner, *Hindu and Muslim Mysticism*, London, 1960, p. 2.
11 *Major Trends in Jewish Mysticism*, 3rd edn, London, 1955, pp. 55–6. For a critique of Scholem on this and similar matters see Moshe Idel, *Kabbalah New Perspectives*, New Haven, Conn., 1988.
12 *Western Mystics*, p. 83.
13 There are a number of solecisms in this note of Baumgardt. Ladi or Liady is in Russia, not in Lithuania; the town is Lubavitch not Lubovitch; the book is usually called either *Likkutey Amarim* or simply *Tanya*, not *Sefer Tanya*. Baumgardt quotes the later chapters of the book but, in fact, there is a detailed exposition of the doctrine of the 'divine soul' right at the beginning of the book, chapter 2, Vilna, 1930, pp. 11f. For the author I have used the more usual form, Shneor Zalman.
14 Cf. J. Skinner, *Genesis*, in ICC, Edinburgh, 1930, pp. 56–7.
15 *De Specialibus Legibus*, IV, 24, English trans. F. H. Coulson and G. H. Whitaker, Loeb Classical Library, 1962, vol. VIII p. 85. For Philo's views on the soul see H. A. Wolfson, *Philo*, Cambridge, Mass., 1948, vol. I, pp. 389–95.
16 *De Legum Allegoria*, I, 13, Loeb Classical Library, vol. I, p. 171.
17 *De Opificio Mundi*, 51, Loeb Classical Library, vol. I, p. 115.
18 See I. Broyde in *JE*, vol. XI, pp. 472–6; George Foot Moore, *Judaism in the First Centuries of the Christian Era*, Cambridge, Mass., 1927, vol. II, index 'Soul', pp. 448–9; K. Kohler, *Jewish Theology*, New York, 1968, pp. 212f.
19 *Shabbat* 152b.
20 *Sifre*, Deuteronomy 306.
21 Midrash Ecclesiastes Rabbah to Ecclesiastes 6:6, Vilna edn, vol. II, p. 17a.
22 *Berakhot* 10a. Cf. Bahya Ibn Pakudah, *Ḥovot ha-Levavot*, *Sha'ar ha-Yihud*, chapter 10, ed. Jerusalem, 1966, p. 87; English trans., *Duties of the Heart*, M. Hyamson, New York, 1941, p. 51.
23 *Ta'anit* 11a–b.
24 See *Rashi*, under *ke-ilu*, and the Tosafists on the passage. The note of the *Maharsha* to this passage is homiletical.
25 See Isaac Husik, *A History of Mediaeval Jewish Philosophy*, New York, 1958, pp. xlv–xlvii. A good popular account of mediaeval thought on the soul is *Aḥad ha-'Am*'s essay on Maimonides entitled *Shilton ha-Sekhel*, Collected Works, Berlin, 1921, vol. IV, pp. 2–11.
26 *Keter Malkhut*, XXIX, trans. Bernard Lewis, London, 1961, p. 49.
27 See Hillel Zeitlin, 'Mafteaḥ le-Sefer ha-Zohar', in *ha-Tekufah*, vol. ix, Warsaw, 1921, pp. 287f, and I. Tishby, *Mishnat ha-Zohar*, vol. II, Jerusalem, 1961, pp. 3–124.
28 Zohar II, 174a.
29 See Scholem, *Major Trends*, p. 241 and notes.
30 *Major Trends*, *ibid.* Cf. R. J. Z. Werblowsky, 'Philo and the Zohar', in *JJS* 10 (1959), 38–9.

31 Ed. C. B. Chavel, Jerusalem, 1959, pp. 33–4.

32 This saying with reference to the divine origin of the soul and its identification with the divine is frequently quoted in the later literature in its semi-Aramaic form, *man de-nafaḥ mi-tokho nafaḥ*. Shneor Zalman of Liady in his *Tanya*, Vilna, 1930, part I, chapter 2, p. 11, quotes it as a saying of the Zohar, but there is no such passage in the Zohar. Chavel in his note to this section of Nahmanides (p. 33) gives the source as the *Sefer ha-Kanah* but fails to give the reference. On the development of this saying see the article by M. Halamish, 'The Origin of a Proverb in Kabbalistic Literature', in *Bar-Ilan Annual*, 13 (1976), 211–23.

33 Commentary to the Pentateuch, Jerusalem, 1970, p. 61.

34 *Berakhot* 10a, see above note 22.

35 Cf. A. Altmann (ed.), 'God and the Self in Jewish Mysticism', in *Judaism*, 3 (1954), 142–6, and the same author's 'The Delphic Maxim in Mediaeval Islam and Judaism', in *Biblical and Other Studies*, ed. A. Altmann, Cambridge, Mass., 1963, pp. 196–232.

36 *Sefer Nishmat Ḥayyim*, Stettin, 1851.

37 *Ibid. Maamar* I, p. 2b.

38 Sulzbach, 1758, part I, *Sha'ar* 1, pp. 3a–4a.

39 Part III, *Sha'ar* 2 and 3, pp. 25b–29b.

40 Part III, *Sha'ar* 2, p. 27b.

41 *Genesis Rabbah*, ed. J. Theodor and H. Albeck, Berlin, 1912, vol. II, p. 985.

42 On Cordovero see my translation with an Introduction and notes of his *Palm Tree of Deborah*, London, 1960. On the Safed circle see Solomon Schechter, *Studies in Judaism*, Second Series, Philadelphia, 1945, pp. 148–81. Cordovero's views on the soul are exceedingly complex. In his *Elimah Rabbati*, Brody, 1881, section III, part 4, chapter 62, p. 151, he states that the *neshamah* is the result of the 'copulation' of *Tiferet* and *Malkhut*, but this is further qualified to suggest an even 'higher' source of the soul. Elsewhere (*Pardes Rimmonim*, Koretz, 1786, *Sha'ar* I, chapter 7, p. 8a) he writes that souls are hewn out from under the Throne of Glory although actually they come from a 'higher' source. (On the mediaeval development of the 'Throne of Glory' as the source of the soul, see Werblowsky, 'Philo and the Zohar', p. 39 note 75.) Cf. *Pardes*, *Sha'ar* VIII, chapter 22, pp. 52a–55a, and the whole of *Sha'ar* XXXI, pp. 162bf.

43 Amsterdam, 1717.

44 *Sha'ar ha-Ahavah*, chapter 3, pp. 67–9.

45 Zohar III, 68a.

46 Hanover, 1612; Frankfurt, 1719.

47 Introduction, par. 1.

48 So far as I have been able to discover, Horowitz is the first author to use the verse in Job to denote the idea that the soul is a portion of God. In *Ḥabad* literature this quotation is very frequent.

49 These are the two lowest degrees of the soul; obviously the highest stage of *neshamah* is included as well.

50 I.e. *Pardes Rimmonim* (quoted above, note 42).
51 Prague, 1616, during the author's lifetime, and Jerusalem, 1850 (?); the only two editions of this fascinating little book.
52 In chapter 8, in the reply to his critics, Horowitz records a further objection to his theory (Prague edn, p. 12a). This is that if every Jewish soul is a part of God it must follow that God has numerous parts, and this is an even greater offence against pure monotheism than the Christian doctrine of the Trinity – 'for believers in the Trinity, even though they speak of the three, say at the same time that there is one', i.e., whereas in the author's view there are allegedly in actuality as many parts of God as there are Jewish souls. Horowitz replies by softening still further the boldness of his concept.
53 E.g. in *Tanya*, Vilna, 1930, part I, chapter 1, pp. 10–11, and chapter 5, p. 19. Cf. M. Teitelbaum, *ha-Rav mi-Ladi*, Warsaw, 1913, vol. II, chapter 6, pp. 127–33.
54 *Tanya*, part I, chapter 2, pp. 11f.
55 *Berakhot* 60b, where it is said that man on rising in the morning should say, 'My God the soul [*neshamah*] which Thou hast placed in me is pure. Thou hast fashioned it in me, Thou didst breathe it into me, and Thou preservest it within me and Thou wilt one day take it from me and restore it to me in time to come. So long as the soul is within me I give thanks unto Thee, O Lord, my God, and the God of my fathers, Sovereign of all worlds, Lord of all souls. Blessed art Thou, O Lord, who restorest souls to dead corpses.' This declaration was adapted as part of the morning service (see Singer's *Prayer Book*, p. 6). See Baer's note (*Siddur 'Avodat Yisrael*, Rödelheim, 1868, p. 39) to the effect that one should pause after the words 'My God' in order to avoid the suggestion that the soul is God! David Abudraham (fourteenth century), in his *Commentary to the Prayer Book*, Lisbon, 1489, Jerusalem, 1959, p. 39, had made the same point centuries before Baer.
56 Actually there is no such passage in the Zohar (see above, note 32).
57 I.e. the semen is drawn from the brain, as was believed before the rise of modern medicine.
58 See Shneor Zalman's *Likkutey Torah*, Genesis, Vilna, 1884 (photocopy Brooklyn, 1976), p. 2, where he remarks that in 'external' contemplation the thought in the mind is that God created the world out of nothing – the world is *yesh* and is created out of *ayin*. This leads to 'inner' contemplation in which the thought is reversed – God is the true *yesh* and He created the world which is really *ayin*. A vivid account of the origin of the divine soul is given in *Tanya*, *Iggeret ha-Teshuvah*, chapters 4 and 5, pp. 186–90. Horowitz, as we have seen, denies that he had ever said that the soul is a portion of *En Sof*; but here (though he does not actually go so far as to say that the soul is a portion of *En Sof*) Shneor Zalman speaks, none the less, of 'the soul of man which derives directly from the category of the inner vitality and influence which *En Sof*, blessed be He, pours out' (p. 187). On the doctrine of the two souls

in *Ḥabad* see the elaborate homily of Menahem Mendel of Lubavitch, the third leader of *Ḥabad* and Shneor Zalman's grandson, in his *Derekh Mitzvotekha*, Poltava, 1911, 'On the Command to be Fruitful and Multiply', pp. 1–8.

59 G. Van der Leeuw, *Religion in Essence and Manifestation*, London, 1938, chapter 43, pp. 299–307.

60 *Tao-teh King*, 11, quoted by Van der Leeuw. On this theme in the mystic life see Underhill, *Mysticism*, pp. 347f, who quotes the following from Rumi's *Divan*:

> This is Love; to fly heaven-ward,
> To rend, every instant, a hundred veils.
> The first moment, to renounce life;
> The last step, to fare without feet.
> To regard this word as invisible,
> Not to see what appears to oneself.

61 Vilna and Grodno, 1824.

62 *Nefesh ha-Ḥayyim*, Gate I, chapters 15–16, pp. 13f. Another non-Hasidic nineteenth-century author who accepts (without qualification) the doctrine of the divine spark is Israel Lipschitz (1782–1860) in his homily, 'Derush Or ha-Ḥayyim', printed at the end of volume IV of his famous Commentary to the Mishnah, *Tiferet Yisrael*, Vilna, 1911, pp. 279f. Lipschitz gives the rather crude illustration of a balloon which receives its shape from the breath of the man who blows it up. Cf. his curious observation, in his Commentary to *Avot*, p. 264b, that only Jews possess the divine spark and this is the real reason for the so-called Jewish appearance: since the face is the soul's window!

63 See my English translation of the *Tract on Ecstasy*, with an Introduction and notes, London, 1963. The best Hebrew text is the rare Warsaw edn, 1868, with notes by the author's disciple, Hillel b. Meir of Poritch.

64 For similar descriptions of mystical prayer, see F. Heiler, *Prayer*, translated and edited by Samuel McComb with the assistance of J. Edgar Park, New York and Oxford, 1958, pp. 190–1.

8 DOES A PERSON'S BODY BELONG TO GOD?

1 The concept of ownership with regard to property is mentioned repeatedly in all the sources but, until fairly recent times, there has been no real analysis of the concept. See Isaac Herzog, *The Main Institutions of Jewish Law*, 2nd edn, London, 1965, vol. I, chapter 4, 'Ownership', pp. 69–95.

2 In fact, a closer look at the Gemara suggests that the 'denial' motif is introduced as an extension of the 'waste' motif, i.e. to show that *bal tashḥit* applies even where the body will be healed later. Cf. the comment of *Tiferet Yisrael* to our Mishnah (*Yakhin*, note 39). It is worth noting that the *Tur* (*Oraḥ Ḥayyim* 620) quotes R Meir ha-Levi, the

Ramah, as ruling, contrary to our Mishnah, that a man *is* permitted to inflict injury on himself (see *Bet Yosef*, note 21).

3 See, e.g., *Ketubot* 31a and freq.

4 In his famous essay on the Shylock case according to the Halakhah, in his *le-Or ha-Halakhah*, Jerusalem, 1959, pp. 310–28, and in his *Sefarim ve-Soferim*, Tel-Aviv, 1959, *Pesakim*, pp. 11–12.

5 *Shulḥan 'Arukh ha-Rav*, New York, 1974, *Nizkey Guf va-Nefesh*, par. 4.

6 The expression that *malkut* is half a death does not occur in the Talmud but see *Sanhedrin* 10a for a comparison of *malkut* with death, and the discussion in *Ketubot* 34b on which is worse, death or *malkut*, Cf. *Bava Metzia*' 95a, 'What difference is there between killing the animal completely and half-killing it?', but that passage is not really relevant.

7 It should be noted that *Radbaz* sums it up by saying that his reason is really inadequate and all one can say is that it is a 'divine decree' not to be questioned. Sevin quotes the Responsa of Joseph Ibn Migash (no. 186) where, Sevin remarks, a similar view is recorded to that of *Radbaz*. But all that Ibn Migash says is that the Torah does not permit a man to give himself pain, which is no more than a paraphrase of the Gemara.

8 For two recent authors with views similar to that of Sevin see I. Rudnik, *Sedey Yitzḥak*, London, 1960, vol. I, pp. 1–7 (where Rudnik discusses whether a Jew is allowed to earn his living as a prizefighter), and Z. Alony, *Toledot Yitzḥak*, London, 1984, pp. 7–16.

9 *Pesaḥim* 90a; *Yevamot* 83b. Cf. R Joseph Engel, *Gilyoney ha-Shas* (Jerusalem, n.d.) to *Yevamot* 47a, who remarks that if a man declares that he is a Gentile he is not allowed to marry a Jewish woman not because of the laws of evidence but because a man can render his own body *which belongs to him* forbidden just as he can place a ban on his property (italics mine).

10 *Kiddushin* 14b. R Joab Weingarten in his *Ḥelkat Yoav*, *Kaba de-Kushyaita*, no. 1, Jerusalem, 1985, vol. I, p. 349, makes the incidental remark that in *Nazir* 61a it is stated that a man's person (*nefesh*) does not belong to him but to God. This is as Sevin holds but is an astonishing statement since the passage in *Nazir* refers explicitly to a slave and not to a free man. Slavery is obviously in a category of its own. There is nothing in the passage to warrant the suggestion that a man's body does not belong to him but to God.

11 R Hayyim Ibn Atar, *Or ha-Ḥayyim* (Jerusalem, n.d.), vol. II, p. 250, to Numbers 16:24 does say that Moses spoke sternly to warn the people to keep away from Korah and his company in order that they should not meet with Korah's fate, even if they themselves did not care whether they lived or died, because the people of Israel are 'God's property' (*nikhsey shamayyim*). This is, however, no more than a pleasant homiletical flourish on the theme that God cares for the community and is not relevant to our question.

9 WORSHIP WITH THE BODY

1 For Bahya see the edition of *Ḥovot ha-Levavot* by P. J. Liebermann, Jerusalem, 1968; the English translation, *Duties of the Heart*, by M. Hyamson, New York, 1941; I. Husik, *A History of Mediaeval Jewish Philosophy*, New York, 1958, chapter 6, pp. 80–105; *Encyclopedia Judaica*, see under 'Bahya', vol. IV, pp. 105–8. The work *Sefer Ḥaredim* by the Kabbalist Eleazar Azikri (1533–1600) lists the precepts to be carried out by each organ of the body: the heart, the eyes, the ear, the mouth, the oesophagus, the nose, the hands, the torso, the feet and the penis. This work has gone into many editions, the best with a commentary by Judah Segal Deutsch entitled *Beer Yehudah*, Jerusalem, 1966. There is also a good deal of material on the theme in the work of Azikri's contemporary, Elijah de Vidas, in his *Reshit Ḥokhmah* (see the edition of H. J. Waldmann, *Reshit Ḥokhmah ha-Shalem*, Jerusalem, 1984, vol. III, index, see under *guf ve-evarim*, pp. 676–81, and *guf u-neshamah*, p. 681).

2 Babylonian Talmud, *Makkot* 23b.

3 *Pesikta de-Rab Kahana*, 12, *ba-ḥodesh ha-shelishi*, ed. B. Mandelbaum, New York, 1962, vol. I, p. 203; English trans., *Pesikta de-Rab Kahana*, by William G. Braude and Israel J. Kapstein, London, 1975, pp. 227–8.

4 On the *Shi'ur Komah* see G. Scholem, *Major Trends in Jewish Mysticism*, 3rd edn, London, 1955, pp. 63–7, and his *Kabbalah*, Jerusalem, 1974, pp. 16–18.

5 *Tikkuney Zohar*, Second Introduction, ed. Reuben Margaliot, Jerusalem, 1964, p. 17a. The translation is mine in my *Jewish Ethics, Philosophy and Mysticism*, New York, 1969, pp. 115–20. In *Zohar Ḥadash* (ed. Reuben Margaliot, Jerusalem, 1964, p. 74a) it is stated that the human body fashioned after the *Sefirot* is the meaning of 'the image of God' in man. Cf. *Ra'ya Mehemna* in Zohar, II, 42a: 'There is no creature that does not have the impression of this name (the Tetragrammaton) pointing to its Creator. The *yod* is the form of every creature's head. The two *heys* (the letter *hey* has the numerical value of five) the five fingers of the right hand and the five fingers of the left. The *vav* is in the form of the torso.' But see *Tikkuney Zohar* (21, p. 48b in the Margaliot edn) that human flesh derives from the leprous skin of the Serpent.

6 *Tikkun* 30 (Margaliot edn, p. 74a).

7 See R Shneor Zalman of Liady, *Tanya*, Vilna, 1930, chapter 23, p. 28a, who quotes this as: 'The 248 precepts are the 248 limbs of the King.' This does seem to be implied but the actual wording of the *Tikkuney Zohar* is, 'Each limb of the King is a precept.'

8 Zohar II, 76a, English translation *The Zohar*, ed. H. Sperling, M. Simon and P. Levertoff, London, 1949, vol. III, p. 230.

9 Babylonian Talmud, *Berakhot* 23a.

10 *Shulḥan 'Arukh, Oraḥ Ḥayyim* 92:1.

11 *Shulḥan 'Arukh, Oraḥ Ḥayyim* 3.

12 *Likkutey Torah*, Lemberg, 1865, *shavu'ot*, p. 54a.
13 Babylonian Talmud, *Berakhot* 60b.
14 *Oraḥ Ḥayyim* 6.
15 *Shulḥan 'Arukh, Oraḥ Ḥayyim* 4 (see Commentaries for the reasons).
16 *Magen Avraham*, on *Shulḥan 'Arukh, Oraḥ Ḥayyim* 4 note 1. Gombiner also refers to Maimonides (*Yad*, *Tefillah* 4:3), who rules that the hands are to be ritually washed before every prayer but before the morning prayer face, hands and feet.
17 Babylonian Talmud, *Shabbat* 50b.
18 Comment of *Rashi*, to the passage.
19 ARN, B, ed. S. Schechter, Vienna, 1887, p. 66; Leviticus Rabbah 34:3.
20 See I. H. Friedmann, *Likkutey Maharih*, Jerusalem, 1970, vol. 1, p. 7a.
21 Babylonian Talmud, *Berakhot* 22a.
22 For the significance of immersion in Hasidism see my *A Tree of Life*, Oxford, 1984, p. 83 and notes, and on annihilation of selfhood see the remarks above pp. 55–6.
23 Babylonian Talmud, *Shabbat* 10a.
24 *Oraḥ Ḥayyim* 91:2.
25 *Oraḥ Ḥayyim* 8.
26 *Oraḥ Ḥayyim* 25.
27 *The Authorised Daily Prayer Book*, ed. Simeon Singer, London, 1962, p. 1.
28 Singer's *Prayer Book*, p. 2.
29 Zohar III, 218b–9a.
30 See Judah Halevi, *Sefer ha-Kuzari*, ed. J. Even-Shemuel (Kaufmann), Tel-Aviv, 1972, II, 79–80; English trans. H. Hirschfeld, *Kitab Al Khazari*, London, 1931.
31 *Oraḥ Ḥayyim* 48:1.
32 note 4.
33 See my *Hasidic Prayer*, London, 1972, pp. 56–9.
34 *Oraḥ Ḥayyim* 61:5.
35 Ecclesiastes Rabbah 7:25.
36 See J. D. Zinger, *Ziv ha-Minhagim*, Jerusalem, 1971, p. 197.
37 *Oraḥ Ḥayyim* 125:2.
38 *Oraḥ Ḥayyim* 95:1.
39 See Friedmann, *Likkutey*, vol. 1, pp. 72a and 86a.
40 Babylonian Talmud, *Berakhot* 34a.
41 *Berakhot* 12a–b.
42 *Berakhot* 28b. Kneeling, on the other hand, is not usually practised during prayer, perhaps in reaction to Christian worship. The practice of resting the head on the left arm during the supplicatory prayer (see *EJ*, under 'Taḥanun', vol. XV, pp. 702–3) now takes this form but originally *nefilat appaim*, 'Falling on the face', meant just that, complete prostration with the face to the ground. Cf. de Vidas, *Reshit Ḥokhmah ha-Shalem, Totzaot Ḥayyim*, vol. III, no. 161, that a man have the intention when falling on his face to give up his life for the sanctification of the divine name.

43 Zohar II, 67a.
44 Jerusalem, 1965. See my *Jewish Mystical Testimonies*, New York, 1977, pp. 180–1. Cf. de Vidas, *Reshit Ḥokhmah, Totzaot Ḥayyim*, vol. III, p. 358, based on Zohar III, 24a that care should be taken not to cross the fingers of the two hands because this is to mingle the *Sefirot* of the left and right. See *Tikkuney Zohar* 13 (ed. Margaliot, p. 27b) that when the hands are clapped together when singing God's praises the Ten *Sefirot* are brought into play.
45 There is an immense literature on this subject. Three articles should be noted in particular: Samuel Krauss, 'The Jewish Rite of Covering the Head', in *HUCA*, 19 (1945–6), 121–68; J. Z. Lauterbach, 'Should One Cover the Head When Participating in Divine Worship?', in CCAR Yearbook, 38 (1928), 586–603; Isaac Rivkind, 'A Responsum of Leo da Modena on Uncovering the Head' (Heb.), in *Louis Ginzberg Jubilee Volume*, New York, 1945, Hebrew section, pp. 401–23.
46 *Teshuvot-Pesakim U-Minhagim*, ed. I. Z. Kahana, Jerusalem, 1957–62, part I, no. 23, p. 53.
47 *Magen Avraham* to *Oraḥ Ḥayyim* 53, note 1. See my *Theology in the Responsa*, London, 1975, index, under 'cripple' for further discussion of this question. Cf. J. H. Bacharach, *Ḥavvot Yair*, Frankfurt, 1699, no. 176, and A. Lewin, Responsa *Avney Ḥefetz*, Munich, 1948.
48 *Oraḥ Ḥayyim* 2.
49 M. Wiener, *Hadrat Panim Zakan*, Brooklyn and New York, 1977.
50 *Oraḥ Ḥayyim* 260.
51 *Oraḥ Ḥayyim* 261:1.
52 *Magen Avraham* to *Oraḥ Ḥayyim* 260, note 3.
53 Cf. *Rashi* to *Berakhot* 62a, under *ta'amey torah*, who observes that in his day people from Eretz Israel would point in the air with the right hand to depict the notes of the Torah cantillation.
54 Leviticus 23:42–3.
55 Babylonian Talmud, *Yevamot* 63b, and see above p. 55.
56 *Even ha-'Ezer* 1:4.
57 For a study of Jewish sex ethics see Louis M. Epstein, *Sex Laws and Customs in Judaism*, New York, 1948, and cf. David M. Feldman, *Marital Relations Birth Control and Abortion in Jewish Law*, New York, 1974.
58 See, e.g., Jacob Emden's Prayer Book, *Siddur Bet Ya'akov*, Lemberg, 1904, pp. 158–60, on marital relations on Sabbath eve, the especially appropriate time according to the Kabbalah to bring down lofty souls into the bodies of children conceived at that time. On the need to adopt the 'missionary position' see Zohar II, 259a.
59 *'Etz Ḥayyim*, Koretz, 1784, Introduction.
60 See *The Holy Letter: A Study in Medieval Sexual Morality*, ed. and trans. Seymour J. Cohen, New York, 1976.
61 *Moreh Nevukhim*, Lemberg, 1886; English trans. S. Pines, *Guide of the Perplexed*, Chicago, Ill., 1963, part II, chapter 36.
62 See Gombiner, *Magen Avraham* to *Oraḥ Ḥayyim* 128, note 19.

63 Leviticus 19:32, interpreted to include a sage in *Kiddushin* 32b.
64 Babylonian Talmud, *Berakhot* 6b.
65 *Yad*, *Yesodey ha-Tora* 4:1, and see above pp. 3–14.
66 For a summary in Hebrew with learned notes see *Zikhron Meir* by Aaron Levine, Toronto, 1985.
67 For Jewish eschatology see my *A Jewish Theology*, London, 1973, pp. 301–22, and see pp. 94–101 in this book.
68 On this see A. Altmann, 'The Delphic Maxim in Medieval Islam and Judaism', in his *Studies in Religious Philosophy and Mysticism*, London, 1969, pp. 1–40.

10 GOD AND PERSONAL FREEDOM

1 Simhah of Vitry, *Maḥzor Vitry*, ed. S. Hurwitz and A. Berliner, Nürnberg, 1923, p. 514, understands the Mishnah to mean that although God sees men doing evil He does not interfere with their choice. See E. Urbach *Ḥazal*, Jerusalem, 1960, pp. 229–30, who remarks that he has found the use of *tzafui*, in the sense of gazing into the future, only in the Amoraic literature, never in the Tannaitic. It is worth noting that the whole of this Mishnah bears all the marks of an interpolation. It has no connection with the previous saying of Rabbi Akiba in the Mishnah nor with that which follows it and it is not prefaced, as they are, with the introduction, 'He used to say'. Furthermore, the meaning of *reshut* is uncertain here. In *Avot* 1:10 and 2:3, *rashut* means the ruling power, i.e. the Roman government. On the other hand, in *Mekhilta*, ed. I. H. Weiss, Vienna, 1865, p. 54b, the saying of our Mishnah *ve-ha-reshut netunah* does occur in connection with the theme of man's freedom of choice. Cf. Charles Taylor's notes to his edition of *Avot*, *Sayings of the Jewish Fathers*, Cambridge, 1900, pp. 152–3.
2 See the writings of Max Kadushin on 'organic thinking', e.g. in his *The Rabbinic Mind*, 2nd edn, New York, 1965. Cf. George Foot Moore, *Judaism in the First Centuries of the Christian Era*, Cambridge, Mass., 1927, p. 454: 'That man is capable of choosing between right and wrong and of carrying his decisions into action was not questioned, nor was any conflict discovered between this freedom of choice with its consequences and the belief that all things are ordained and brought to pass by God in accordance with his wisdom and his righteous and benevolent will. The theological problem of the freedom of the will in relation to the doctrine of divine providence and the omniscience of God did not emerge until the 10th century, when Jewish thinkers like Saadia (d. 942) heard around them on every hand the Moslem controversies over predestination.' Saadia Gaon, (*Beliefs and Opinions*, IV, 4) touches on the problem and simply says that God knows the final outcome, without elaborating on the matter.
3 Maimonides here refers to his argument that man is free as stated in his *Eight Chapters*, Maimonides' Introduction to *Avot*.

4 Maimonides elaborates on this theme of the total difference between divine and human knowledge in his *Guide of the Perplexed*, III, 20.
5 In that case, why call it knowledge? Maimonides would probably reply, in order to distinguish it from its contrary, ignorance. See Maimonides' development of his doctrine of negative attributes, *Guide of the Perplexed*, I, 51–60.
6 *Milḥamot Adonai*, Riva di Trento, 1560, III, 6.
7 *A History of Mediaeval Jewish Philosophy*, New York, 1958, pp. 345–6. Centuries later, a throughgoing religious determinist emerged inthe person of the Hasidic master, Mordecai Joseph of Izbica (d. 1854). This thinker's religious determinism is based not so much on the question of God's foreknowledge as on the question of how there can be any human freedom since God is in complete control of His universe, even, according to Mordecai Joseph, of man's moral life. Man, he holds, has been given by God the *illusion* that he is free, otherwise he could not worship God. For an acute analysis of the thought of this master (wrongly stated to be Joseph Mordecai instead of Mordecai Joseph) see J. G. Weiss, 'The Religious Determinism of Joseph Mordecai of Izbica' (Heb.), in S. Ettinger *et al.* (eds.), *The Baer Jubilee Volume*, Jerusalem, 1960, pp. 447–53. For Mordecai Joseph it is not so much a question of God's knowledge versus human free-will, as of God's will versus human will.
8 *Or Adonai*, Vienna, 1859, 4:5.
9 Responsa *Ribash*, no. 45, photocopy of I. H. Daiches (ed.), New York, 1943.
10 No. 118.
11 *Magen Avot*, Leghorn, 1763.
12 *Sanhedrin* 90b.
13 For Jewish thinkers who discuss the Eternal Now, see my *A Jewish Theology*, London, 1973, pp. 86–92.
14 *Or ha-Ḥayyim* (various editions) to Genesis 6:6. Ibn Atar seeks to read this idea into Maimonides and he takes strong issue with *Raabad*, saying, 'May God forgive him.' This is said to have aroused the ire of Mordecai Joseph of Izbica (mentioned above note 7) who is reported to have remarked, 'He also puts his nose into everything', i.e. he, too, is trying to 'get in on the act'. This remark is said to be one of the reasons for the break between Mordecai Joseph and his master, the Kotzker Rebbe (see A. Markus, *ha-Ḥasidut*, Hebrew trans. M. Shenfeld, Tel-Aviv, 1954, p. 244).
15 *'Amud ha-'Avodah*, Josephof, 1883, pp. 221–5.
16 From the mediaeval work, *Ben ha-Melekh ve-ha-Nazir*.
17 Jerusalem Talmud *Ḥagigah* 1:7; Lamentations Rabbah, Introduction, 2.
18 *Yesod ha-Emunah*, Josephof, 1883, pp. 141–59.
19 *Beney Yissakhar*, *Tishri*, *Maamar* 7:5, various editions, and Israel, n.p., n.d.

20 *Sha'arey ha-Yiḥud ve-ha-Emunah*, Shklov, 1820, vol. II, *Sha'ar* 3, chapter 38. See my study of Aaron's thought: *Seeker of Unity*, London, 1966, pp. 103–5.

21 *Or Sameaḥ* to Maimonides' *Mishneh Torah*, various editions, pp. 12a–14a.

22 *Shi'urey Da'at*, Tel-Aviv, 1953, vol. II, Lecture 8, pp. 93–103, delivered originally as a lecture in the Yeshivah of Telz in 1928.

11 IMMORTALITY

1 S. W. Baron, *A Social and Religious History of the Jews*, 2nd edn, vol. I, New York, 1952, p. 357 note 5.

2 See *ERE*, vol. IV, pp. 243–4, and G. F. Moore, *History of Religions*, Edinburgh, 1914, vol. I, pp. 228f.

3 W. B. Emery, *Archaic Egypt*, London, 1961, p. 129.

4 See Ezekiel Kaufmann, *The Religion of Israel*, translated and abridged by Moshe Greenberg, London, 1961, pp. 311–16, and Kaufmann's original Hebrew work, *Toledot ha-Emunah ha-Yisraelit*, Tel-Aviv, 1952, vol. II, Book 2, chapter 17, pp. 544–56.

5 See, e.g., Exodus 12:15; Leviticus 18:29; Leviticus 20:4–5 and Hastings, *Dictionary of the Bible*, Edinburgh, 1963, p. 190.

6 See, e.g., Numbers 16:30; Isaiah 35:18–19; Amos 9:2 and Hastings, *Dictionary*, under 'Sheol', p. 906.

7 See R. H. Charles, *A Critical History of the Doctrine of a Future Life*, London, 1899, chapters 5–8, pp. 162–305, and Herbert Loewe, 'Judaism', in *ERE*, vol. VII, pp. 581–609.

8 Mishnah *Berakhot* 9:5.

9 Josephus, *Antiquities*, Book XVIII, chapter 2, Works, trans. H. St John Thackeray, R. Marcus and I. H. Feldman, in Loeb Classical Library, Cambridge, Mass., 1929–65.

10 But see David Neumark, *Toledot ha-'Ikkarim be-Yisrael*, Odessa, 1912, chapter 6, pp. 165–75, that Josephus is only stating his own opinion and in reality the Sadducees did believe in the immortality of the soul but not in the resurrection of the dead.

11 H. A. Wolfson, *Philo*, Cambridge, Mass., 1948, vol. I, chapter 7, section 5: 'The Immortality of the Soul', pp. 395–413, and see Charles, *Critical History*, p. 260, that since Philo held that matter was incurably evil there could be no resurrection of the body.

12 See H. Albeck's edition of the Mishnah, Jerusalem and Tel-Aviv, 1960, *hashlamot*, note to Mishnah *Sanhedrin* 10:1.

13 *Kiddushin* 40b (cf. ARN, XXXIX).

14 See, e.g., *Avot* 5:20 for the only reference to *Gan Eden* in the Tannaitic literature and, e.g., *Berakhot* 28b; *Shabbat* 119b; *Nedarim* 39b; *Ta'anit* 31a; *Sanhedrin* 102b for the Amoraic literature.

15 See, e.g., for the Tannaitic literature *Avot* 1:5 and 5:20; '*Eduyot* 2:10; *Kiddushin* 4:14; and for the Amoraic literature, e.g., *Berakhot* 15b; '*Eruvin* 19a; *Nedarim* 8b.

16 *Berakhot* 18a–19a.
17 See, e.g., *Bava Kama* 92a; *Bava Metzia*ʿ 86a.
18 *Emunot ve-De*ʿ*ot* VI: 1.
19 *Emunot ve-De*ʿ*ot* VI: 4.
20 *Emunot ve-De*ʿ*ot* VI: 4.
21 *Shabbat* 152a.
22 *Emunot ve-De*ʿ*ot* VI: 7.
22 *Emunot ve-De*ʿ*ot* VI: 8.
23 *Emunot ve-De*ʿ*ot* VII: 1.
24 *Emunot ve-De*ʿ*ot* VII: 1–7.
25 *Emunot ve-De*ʿ*ot* VII: 8 to IX: 8.
26 *Emunot ve-De*ʿ*ot* IX: 10.
27 Maimonides' views are to be found especially in his *Guide of the Perplexed*, III, 27, 51–2, 54, and in his *Mishneh Torah*, *Teshuvah* 8: 3.
28 Commentary to the Mishnah to *Sanhedrin* 10: 1.
29 See *Maamar Teḥiat ha-Metim*, *Maimonides' Treatise on the Resurrection*, ed. Joshua Finkel, New York, 1939.
30 *Mishneh Torah*, *Teshuvah* 8: 3–8.
31 *Mishneh Torah*, *Melakhim* 12: 4.
32 In Collected writings, ed. C. B. Chavel, Jerusalem, 1964, vol. II, *Sha*ʿ*ar ha-Gemul*. See my *A Jewish Theology*, London, 1973, pp. 313–15.
33 *Mishneh Torah*, *Teshuvah* 8: 2.
34 *Berakhot* 17b.
35 Zohar I, 135b.
36 Zohar III, 169b.
37 *Zohar Ḥadash*, *noaḥ*, 21a.
38 Zohar I, 235a.
39 *Nahama de-kisufa*, see Luzzatto's *Kelaḥ Pitḥey Ḥokhmah*, Jerusalem, 1961, no. 4 (p. 7a) and Luzzatto's note. Cf. Zohar I, 4a: 'Happy is he who enters here without shame' (*kesufa*).
40 Ed. with trans. by Mordecai M. Kaplan, Philadelphia, 1936.
41 See, e.g., Collected Writings of Joseph Seliger (Heb.), ed. Leah Seliger, Jerusalem, 1939, pp. 71–95, and J. H. Hertz, *The Authorised Daily Prayer Book*, London, 1947, p. 133, on the reference to the revival of the dead: 'He awakes the dead to new life. This emphatic statement concerning the resurrection was directed especially against the worldlings, who disputed the deathlessness of the soul, its return to God, and its continued separate existence after its reunion with the Divine Source of being.' And see Hertz's remark on p. 255: 'Maimonides and Hallevi make the doctrine of *teḥiat ha-metim*, lit. "revival of the dead", identical with that of the immortality of the soul, and explain the Talmudic sayings to the contrary as figurative language.'
42 *Bava Kama* 92a; *Bava Metzia*ʿ *86a*.
43 *Pesaḥim* 50a.
44 So Soncino, p. 239, but *Rashi* understands *itnegid* to mean that he actually died.

45 B. M. Lewin (ed.) *Otzar ha-Geonim*, *Pesaḥim*, Jerusalem, 1931, p. 71.
46 *Shabbat* 55a.
47 *Bava Batra* 75a.
48 Zohar I, 129b.
49 Zohar I, 130a, obviously based on the *Bava Batra* passage.
50 *'Uktzin* 3:12.
51 *Sanhedrin* 100a.
52 Ecclesiastes Rabbah 12:5. Cf. *Shabbat* 152a: 'Every *tzaddik* has an abode in accordance with the honour due to him.'
53 Exodus Rabbah 52:3. Cf. the parallel passage in *Ta'anit* 25a where the hero of the tale is R Hanina b. Dosa and where the other saints sit at tables with three legs while R Hanina and his wife sit at a table with only two legs.
54 *Ḥagigah* 15a. Cf. Mishnah *Sanhedrin* 10:1 for the idea of a 'portion' (*ḥelek*) in the World to Come and see Midrash Leviticus Rabbah 27:1 that each saint has his own 'Gan Eden'.
55 *Ta'anit* 31a.
56 For Maimonides' view see above p. 77. Maimonides understands the 'crowns' on the heads of the saints in Paradise as the knowledge of God which they had attained while on earth.
57 E. de Vidas, *Reshit Ḥokhmah ha-Shalem*, ed. H. J. Waldmann, Jerusalem, 1984, *Sha'ar ha-Yirah* 7:11 and *Sha'ar ha-Ahavah* 6:64.
58 *Sha'ar ha-Ahavah* 6:54.
59 Zohar I, 219a.
60 *Sha'ar ha-Ahavah* 6:57.
61 *Sha'ar ha-Kedushah* 4:21.
62 *Maggid Mesharim*, Amsterdam, 1704, pp. 1b–2a; see my *Jewish Mystical Testimonies*, New York, 1977, pp. 104–10, and on Karo and his diary generally, R. J. Z. Werblowsky, *Joseph Karo*, Oxford, 1962.
63 M. S. Kasher's anthologies, all published in Jerusalem, are: *Perakim be-Torat ha-Ḥasidut*, 1968, abbrev. PTH.; *Perakim be-Mishnat ha-Ḥasidut*, 1970, abbrev. P Mish H; *Perakim be-Maḥashevet ha-Ḥasidut*, 1972, abbrev. PMH; *'Iyyunim be-Maḥashevet ha-Ḥasidut*, 1974, abbrev. IMH; *Netivot be-Maḥashevet ha-Ḥasidut*, 1975, abbrev. NH; *Mesillot be-Maḥashevet ha-Ḥasidut*, 1977, abbrev. MMH; *Shevilim be-Maḥashevet ha-Ḥasidut*, 1978, abbrev. SH; *'Erkhey ha-Ḥasidut*, 1979, abbrev. EH.
64 *Torat Avot*, ed. 'Bet Avraham', Jerusalem, 1971, p. 203, no. 9; Kasher, PMH, pp. 69–70.
65 *Tzafenat Paneaḥ*, Koretz, 1782, p. 59b; Kasher, PMH, p. 21.
66 *Bet Ya'akov*, Jerusalem, 1975, p. 30a; Kasher, MMH, pp. 134–5.
67 *Pesaḥim* 8a.
68 *'Atarah le-Rosh Tzaddik*, Warsaw, 1895, p. 129; Kasher, IMH, pp. 42–3.
69 *'Arvey Naḥal*, Warsaw, 1905, p. 90b; Kasher, P Mish H, pp. 37–8.
70 *Bava Batra* 75a.
71 *Mey ha-Shiloaḥ*, Brooklyn and New York, 1973, p. 33b.
72 *Toledot Ya'akov Yosef*, Koretz, 1780, photocopy Jerusalem, 1966, *naso*, p. 120b; Kasher, PTH, p. 51.

73 *Likkutey Torah*, Vilna. 1884, photocopy Brooklyn, 1976, p. 1; Kasher, NH, p. 22.
74 *Torah Or*, Brooklyn, 1955, p. 81a; Kasher, EH, p. 152.
75 *No'am Elimelekh*, ed. G. Nigal, Jerusalem, 1978, *terumah*, pp. 251–2; Kasher, SH, p. 80.
76 With English translation in Menahem G. Glenn, *Israel Salanter*, New York, 1953, pp. 127–55.
77 Translation of Glenn, *ibid.* p. 128.
78 *Ibid.*, p. 130.
79 The standard work on the Musar movement is Dov Katz, *Tenu'at ha-Musar*, Tel-Aviv, 1958, and Katz's companion volume, *Pulmos ha-Musar*, Jerusalem, 1972. *Torat ha-Musar*, ed. David Zeritzski, Tel-Aviv, n.d., is an anthology of the teachings of the Musarists. Even a cursory glance at these works is sufficient to see how strong the individual thrust is in the movement.
80 *Mikhtav me-Eliyahu*, ed. A. Karmel and A. Halpern, Bene Berak, 1977, vol. 1, pp. 284–94.
81 *Mikhtav me-Eliyahu*, pp. 291–2.
82 *Mikhtav me-Eliyahu*, pp. 296–305.
83 English trans. by Charles Cullen, London, 1789.
84 Translated William W. Hallo, London, 1971: see index 'Immortality'.

12 CONCLUSION: A QUESTION OF EMPHASIS

1 E. B. Borowitz, *Choices in Modern Jewish Thought: A Partisan Guide*, New York, 1983, p. 243–72.
2 On p. 268, Borowitz, while praising my books *Principles of the Jewish Faith* and *A Jewish Theology* observes that the issue of the place and form of proper dissent in Judaism constitutes the critical unresolved issue in these works. I admit that my main concern was historical but I have now considered the contemporary question in *God Torah Israel: Traditionalism without Fundamentalism*, Cincinnati, 1990.
3 Page 249.
4 Sol Roth, *Halakhah and Politics: The Jewish Idea of a State*, New York, 1988.
5 David Hartman, *A Living Covenant: The Innovative Spirit in Traditional Judaism*, New York, 1985.
6 Pages 117–28.
7 Page 125.
8 Pages 93–103.
9 Pages 104–16.
10 Pages 104–5. Cf. my observations on pp. 31–2.
11 Hartman, *Living Covenant*, pp. 60–88.
12 For Erich Fromm's thought see his *You Shall Be as Gods*, Greenwich, Conn., 1966; and his *Psychoanalysis and Religion*, New Haven, Conn., 1950.
13 Isaiah Leibowitz, *Emunah Historia ve-'Arakhin*, Jerusalem, 1982.

14 J. B. Soloveitchik, *Halakhic Man*, trans. Lawrence Kaplan, Philadelphia, 1983; Soloveitchik, 'The Lonely Man of Faith', in *Tradition*, 7:2 (Spring, 1978), pp. 5–67.
15 Hartman, *Living Covenant*, p. 13.
16 *Ibid.*, p. 302.
17 Title of chapter in Ralph Barton Perry, *Puritanism and Democracy*, quoted in Milton K. Munitz (ed.), *A Modern Introduction to Ethics*, Glencoe, Ill., 1958.
18 Perry in Munitz, *Introduction to Ethics*, p. 477.
19 *Ibid.*, p. 496.
20 *Ibid.*, p. 478.
21 J. S. Mill, *On Liberty*, Everyman, London, 1924.
22 Kathleen Nott, *The Good Want Power: An Essay on the Psychological Possibilities of Liberalism*, London, 1977, pp. 92–112.
23 The term for society in general in relation to the individual, *kelal*, is also of late vintage. Cf. the Yiddish saying, '*Kelal Yisrael* [the generality of Israel] takes precedence over Reb Yisrael [Mr Israel].'
24 Søren Kierkegaard, *Fear and Trembling* and *A Sickness unto Death*, trans. Walter Lowrie, New York, 1954.
25 'The Problem of the '*Akedah* in Jewish Thought', in Robert L. Perkins (ed.), *Kierkegaard's Fear and Trembling*, Birmingham, Ala., 1981, pp. 1–9, and see above p. 8.
26 On the religious question see further the essays in *Religion and Morality*, ed. Gene Outka and John P. Reeder, Jr, New York, 1973; and on the general question William Lillie, *An Introduction to Ethics*, London, 1948, chapter 14, 'The Individual and Society', pp. 239–58.
27 See Frederick Copleston, *Contemporary Philosophy*, London, 1956, pp. 105–9; Robert G. Olson, *An Introduction to Existentialism*, New York, 1963, pp. 162–78; James Collins, *The Existentialists: A Critical Study*, Chicago, 1963, pp. 3–18, and above pp. 7–9.

Bibliography

CLASSICAL WORKS

The Bible: *Mikraot Gedolot*, various editions. Translations: AV; Jewish Publication Society of America, Philadelphia, 1978
Mishnah, ed. H. Albeck, Jerusalem and Tel-Aviv, 1960; trans. H. Danby, *The Mishnah*, Oxford, 1933
Babylonian Talmud, Romm edn, Vilna, trans. into English and ed. I. Epstein, Soncino Press, London, 1952
Palestinian Talmud, Romm edn, Vilna: Krotoschin, 1866
Tosefta, ed. M. S. Zuckermandel, Pasewalk, 1881
Sifra, ed. I. H. Weiss, Vienna, 1862
Sifre, ed. M. Friedmann, Vienna, 1864; ed. L. Finkelstein and H. S. Horowitz, New York, 1969
Avot de-Rabbi Nathan, ed. S. Schechter, Vienna, 1887
Midrash Rabbah, Romm edn, Vilna, 1911
Midrash Genesis Rabbah, ed. J. Theodor and H. Albeck, Berlin, 1912
Mekhilta, ed. I. H. Weiss, Vienna, 1865
Pesikta de-Rab Kahana, ed. B. Mandelbaum, New York, 1962; English trans. William G. Braude and Israel J. Kapstein, London, 1975
Tanna de-Ve Eliyahu, ed. M. Friedmann, Jerusalem, 1960; English trans. William G. Braude and Israel J. Kapstein, Philadelphia, 1981
Yalkut Shime'oni, Warsaw, 1876
Zohar, ed. R. Margaliot, Jerusalem, 1964
Tikkuney Zohar, ed. R. Margaliot, Jerusalem, 1964
Zohar Ḥadash, ed. R. Margaliot, Jerusalem, 1964
The Zohar in English trans. by H. Sperling, M. Simon and P. Levertoff, London, 1949
Meah Berakhot, Amsterdam, 1687

ENCYCLOPAEDIAS, DICTIONARIES AND JOURNALS

Bar-Ilan Annual, Ramat-Gan
Conservative Judaism, New York
Dictionary of the Bible, ed. J. Hastings, revised F. C. Grant and H. H. Rowley, Edinburgh, 1963

Encyclopedia of Religion and Ethics, ed. James Hastings, Edinburgh, 1908
Encyclopedia Judaica, Jerusalem, 1972
Entzyklopedia Talmudit, Jerusalem, 1947–
Hebrew Union College Annual, Cincinnati
Jewish Encyclopedia, New York and London, 1916
Journal of Jewish Studies, Oxford
Judaism, New York
Tarbitz, Jerusalem
Universal Jewish Encyclopedia, New York, 1939–43

OTHER WORKS

Aaron of Starosselje, *Sha'arey ha-Yiḥud ve-ha-Emunah*, Shklov, 1820
Abudraham, David, *Commentary to the Prayer Book* (Heb.), Lisbon, 1489; Jerusalem, 1959
Aḥad ha-'Am ('Asher Ginzberg'), Collected Works, *'Al Parashat Derakhim*, Berlin, 1921; English trans. Leon Simon, *Essays, Letters, Memoirs – Ahad ha-Am*, Oxford, 1946
Albert, A. M., *Ma'aser Kesafim*, Jerusalem, 1977
Albo, Joseph, *Sefer ha-'Ikkarim*. I. Husik, Philadelphia, 1944
Alexander Süsskind of Grodno, *Yesod ve-Shoresh ha-'Avodah*, Jerusalem, 1965
Alony, Z., *Toledot Yitzḥak*, London, 1984
Altmann, Alexander (ed.), *Biblical and Other Studies*, Cambridge, Mass., 1963
'God and the Self in Jewish Mysticism', in *Judaism*, 3 (1954), 142–6
'The Delphic Maxim in Medieval Islam and Judaism', in A. Alexander, *Studies in Religious Philosophy and Mysticism*, London, 1969
Ancelot-Hustache, Jeanne, *Master Ekhart*, trans. Hilda Graef, 'Men of Wisdom' Series, London, 1957
Azikri, Eleazar, *Sefer Ḥaredim*, ed. with Commentary *Beer Yehudah* by J. S. Deutsch, Jerusalem, 1966
Bacharach, Jair Hayyim, Responsa *Ḥavvot Yair*, Frankfurt, 1699
Baer, S., *Siddur 'Avodat Yisrael*, Rödelheim, 1868
Bahya Ibn Asher, Commentary to the Pentateuch, Amsterdam, 1726; ed. C. D. Chavel, Jerusalem, 1970
Bahya Ibn Pakudah, *Ḥovot ha-Levavot*, ed. P. Liebermann, Jerusalem, 1968, English trans. M. Hyamson, *Duties of the Heart*, New York, 1941
Baron, S. W., *The Jewish Community*, Philadelphia, 1945
A Social and Religious History of the Jews, 2nd edn, vol. I, New York, 1952, vol. VIII, New York, 1958
Baruch of Kossov, *'Amud ha-'Avodah*, Josephof, 1883
Yesod ha-Emunah, Josephof, 1883
Baumgardt, David, *Great Western Mystics*, New York, 1961
Bergmann, J. *ha-Tzedakah be-Yisrael*, Jerusalem, 1975
Berlin, Naftali Zvi Yehudah, *Ha'amek Davar*, New York, 1972
'Bet Avraham' (ed.), *Torat Avot*, Jerusalem, 1971

Blidstein, Gerald, *Honor Thy Father and thy Mother*, New York, 1975
Bloch, J. L., *Shi'urey Da'at*, Tel-Aviv, 1953
Borowitz, E. B., *Choices in Modern Jewish Thought: A Partisan Guide*, New York, 1983
Brook, Stephen, *The Club*, London, 1989
Broyde, I., 'Soul', in *JE*, vol. XI, pp. 472–6
Buber, Martin, *Tales of the Hasidim*, New York, 1947–8
Chajes, Z. H., Notes to the Talmud in the Romm edn, Vilna
Charles, R. H., *A Critical History of the Doctrine of a Future Life*, London, 1899
Chen, Abraham, *be-Malkhut ha-Yahadut*, Jerusalem, 1959
Cohen, Arthur A., and Mendes-Flohr, Paul (eds.), *Contemporary Jewish Religious Thought*, New York, 1987
Cohn, H. H., 'Ḥerem', in *EJ*, vol. VIII, pp. 344–55
'Suicide', in *EJ*, vol. XV, pp. 489–91
Collins, James, *The Existentialists: A Critical Study*, Chicago, 1963
Colon, Joseph, Responsa *Maharik*, Warsaw, 1884
Copleston, Frederick, *Contemporary Philosophy*, London, 1956
Cordovero, Moses, *Elimah Rabbati*, Brody, 1881
Pardes Rimmonim, Koretz, 1786
Tomer Devorah, Jerusalem, 1975; English trans. L. Jacobs, *The Palm Tree of Deborah*, London, 1960
Crescas, Hasdai, *Or Adonai*, Vienna, 1859
Dessler, E. E., *Mikhtav me-Eliyahu*, ed. A. Karmel and A. Halpern, Bene Berak, 1977
de Vidas, Elijah, *Reshit Ḥokhmah*, Amsterdam, 1717; ed. H. J. Waldmann, *Reshit Ḥokhmah ha-Shalem*, Jerusalem, 1984
Dov Baer of Lubavitch, *Kunteros ha-Hitpa'alut*, Warsaw, 1868; English trans. L. Jacobs, *Tract on Ecstasy*, London, 1963
Dov Baer, Maggid of Meserich, *Or Torah*, Brooklyn, 1969
Duran, Simeon b. Zemah, *Magen Avot*, Leghorn, 1763
Edels, Samuel Eliezer (*Maharsha*), in Vilna, Romm edn of Talmud
Eibshütz, D. S., *'Arvey Naḥal*, Warsaw, 1905
Elimelech of Lizensk, *No'am Elimelekh*, ed. G. Nigal, Jerusalem, 1978
Emden, Jacob, *Siddur Bet Ya'akov*, Lemberg, 1904
Emery, W. B., *Archaic Egypt*, London, 1961
Engel, Joseph, *Gilyoney ha-Shas*, Jerusalem, n.d.
Epstein, J., *Mitzvot ha-Bayit*, New York, 1972
Epstein, Louis M., *Sex Laws and Customs in Judaism*, New York, 1948
Epstein, Y. M., *'Arukh ha-Shulḥan*, Pietrikow, 1905
Ettinger, S., Baron, S., Dinur, B. and Heilpern, I. (eds.), *The Baer Jubilee Volume*, Jerusalem, 1960
Feldman, David M., *Marital Relations Birth Control and Abortion in Jewish Law*, New York, 1974
Fleckeles, Eliezer, *Teshuvah me-Ahavah*, Prague, 1809–21
Friedmann, I. H., *Likkutey Mahariḥ*, Jerusalem, 1970
Fromm, Erich, *You Shall Be as Gods*, Greenwich, Conn., 1966

Psychoanalysis and Religion, New Haven, Conn., 1950
Fuchs, I. J., *ha-Tefillah be-Tzibbur*, Jerusalem, 1978
Gabirol, Solomon Ibn, *Keter Malkhut*, trans. Bernard Lewis, London, 1961
Gersonides, Levi, *Milḥamot Adonai*, Riva di Trento, 1560
Ginzberg, Louis, *Louis Ginzberg Jubilee Volume*, New York, 1945
Glenn, Menahem G., *Israel Salanter*, New York, 1953
Gombiner, Abraham, *Magen Avraham*, in *Shulḥan 'Arukh, Oraḥ Ḥayyim*, various editions
Green, Arthur (ed.), *Jewish Spirituality*, vol. II, New York, 1987
Greenberg, M., *Biblical Prose Prayers*, Berkeley, Calif., 1983
Halamish, M., 'The Origin of a Proverb in Kabbalistic Literature' (Heb.), in *Bar-Ilan Annual*, 13 (1976), 211–23
Halevi, Judah, *Sefer ha-Kuzari*, ed. J. Even-Shemuel (Kaufmann), Tel-Aviv, 1972; English trans. H. Hirschfeld, *Kitab Al Khazari*, London, 1931
Hartman, David, *A Living Covenant: The Innovative Spirit in Traditional Judaism*, New York, 1985
Hartshorne, C., and Reese, William L. (eds.), *Philosophers Speak of God*, Chicago, Ill., 1953
Hayyim of Volozhyn, *Nefesh ha-Ḥayyim*, Vilna and Grodno, 1824
Ruaḥ Ḥayyim, Vilna, 1859
Heiler, F., *Prayer*, trans. and ed. Samuel McComb, with the assistance of J. Edgar Park, New York and Oxford, 1958
Heller, Yom Tov Lippmann, *Tosafot Yom Tov*, various editions
Hertz, J. H., *The Authorised Daily Prayer Book*, London, 1947
Pentateuch and Haftorahs, London, 1960
Herzog, Isaac, *The Main Institutions of Jewish Law*, 2nd edn, London, 1965
Heschel, Susannah (ed.), *On Being a Jewish Feminist*, New York, 1983
Hillmann, D. Z., *Iggerot ha-Rav Ba'al ha-Tanya*, Jerusalem, 1953
Horowitz, Isaiah, *Sheney Luḥot ha-Berit*, Amsterdam, 1653; Jerusalem, 1963
Horowitz, Pinhas Elijah, *Sefer ha-Berit*, Warsaw, 1881
Horowitz, Shabbetai Sheftel, *Nishmat Shabbetai ha-Levi*, Prague, 1616; Jerusalem, 1950 (?)
Shefa' Tal, Hanover, 1612; Frankfurt, 1719
Hughes, H. Maldwyn, *The Ethics of Jewish Apocryphal Literature*, London, n.d.
Husik, Isaac, *A History of Mediaeval Jewish Philosophy*, New York, 1958
Huxley, Aldous, *The Perennial Philosophy*, London, 1958
Ibn Abi Zimra, David, *Radbaz*, Commentary to Maimonides' *Mishneh Torah*, various editions
Ibn Adret, Solomon, Responsa *Rashba*, Lemberg, 1811
Ibn Atar, Hayyim, *Or ha-Ḥayyim*, Jerusalem, n.d.
Ibn David, Abraham, Strictures to Maimonides' *Mishneh Torah*, various editions
Ibn Ezra, Abraham, Biblical Commentaries, various editions
Ibn Migash, Joseph, Responsa, Warsaw, 1870
Idel, Moshe, *Kabbalah New Perspectives*, New Haven, Conn., 1988

Isserles, Moses, Glosses to the *Shulḥan 'Arukh*, various editions
Jacob b. Asher, *Arba'ah Turim*, various editions
Jacob Joseph of Pulonnoye, *Toledot Ya'akov Yosef*, Koretz, 1780, photocopy, Jerusalem, 1966
Tzafenat Paneaḥ, Koretz, 1782
Jacob Zevi of Parasov, *'Atarah le-Rosh Tzaddik*, Warsaw, 1895
Jacobs, Louis, 'Divine Foreknowledge and Human Free Will', in *Conservative Judaism*, 34 (Sept./Oct. 1980), 4–16
'The Doctrine of the "Divine Spark" in Man in Jewish Sources', in R. Loewe (ed.), *Studies...*, pp. 87–114
God Torah Israel: Traditionalism without Fundamentalism, Cincinnati, 1990
Hasidic Prayer, London, 1972
Jewish Ethics, Philosophy and Mysticism, New York, 1969
Jewish Mystical Testimonies, New York, 1977
A Jewish Theology, London, 1973
Jewish Values, London, 1960, reproduced in *Contemporary Jewish Ethics*, ed. M. M. Kellner, New York, 1978, pp. 1175–86
'Judaism and Membership', in J. Kent and R. Murray (eds.), *Intercommunion..., pp.* 141–53
Principles of the Jewish Faith, 2nd edn, Northvale and London, 1988
'The Problem of the '*Akedah* in Jewish Thought', in Robert L. Perkins (ed.), *Kierkegaard's Fear and Trembling*, pp. 1–9
Seeker of Unity, London, 1966
Theology in the Responsa, London, 1975
A Tree of Life, Oxford, 1984
Josephus, Works, trans. H. St John Thackeray, R. Marcus and I. H. Feldman, in Loeb Classical Library, Cambridge, Mass., 1929–65
Judah he-Hasid, *Sefer Ḥasidim*, ed. R. Margaliot, Jerusalem, 1973; ed. J. Wistinetzki, Frankfurt, 1924
Kadushin, Max, *The Rabbinic Mind*, 2nd edn, New York, 1965
Kagan, Meir Simhah, *Or Sameaḥ*, various editions
Karo, Joseph, *Bet Yosef* to *Tur*, various editions
Kesef Mishneh to Maimonides' *Mishneh Torah*, various editions
Maggid Mesharim, Amsterdam, 1704
Kasher, M. S., *'Iyyunim be-Maḥashevet ha-Ḥasidut*, Jerusalem, 1974
'Erkhey ha-Ḥasidut, Jerusalem, 1979
Mesillot be-Maḥashevet ha-Ḥasidut, Jerusalem, 1977
Netivot be-Maḥashevet ha-Ḥasidut, Jerusalem, 1975
Perakim be-Maḥashevet ha-Ḥasidut, Jerusalem, 1972
Perakim be-Mishnat ha-Ḥasidut, Jerusalem, 1970
Perakim be-Torat ha-Ḥasidut, Jerusalem, 1968
Shevilim be-Maḥashevet ha-Ḥasidut, Jerusalem, 1978
Katz, Dov, *Pulmos ha-Musar*, Jerusalem, 1972
Tenu'at ha-Musar, Tel-Aviv, 1958
Katz, Jacob, 'Though he Sinned he Remains an Israelite' (Heb.), in *Tarbitz*, 27 (1958), 203–47

Kaufmann, Ezekiel, *Toledot ha-Emunah ha-Yisraelit*, Tel-Aviv, 1952, trans. and abridged Moshe Greenberg, *The Religion of Israel*, London, 1961
Kaufmann, Walter (ed.), *Religion from Tolstoy to Camus*, New York, 1961
Kellner, M. M. (ed.), *Contemporary Jewish Ethics*, New York, 1978
Kent, J., and Murray, R. (eds.), *Intercommunion and Church Membership*, London, 1973
Kierkegaard, Søren, *The Last Years Journals 1853–55*, ed. and trans. Ronald Gregor Smith, London, 1965
Fear and Trembling and *A Sickness unto Death*, trans. Walter Lowrie, New York, 1954
Kimhi, David, Commentary to the Bible in *Mikraot Gedolot*, various editions
Kohler, K., *Jewish Theology*, New York, 1968
Krauss, Samuel, 'The Jewish Rite of Covering the Head', in *HUCA*, 19 (1945–6), 121–68
Lauterbach, J. Z., 'Should One Cover the Head When Participating in Divine Worship?', in Central Conference of American Rabbis (CCAR) Yearbook, 38 (1928), 586–603
Leibowitz, Isaiah, *Emunah Historia ve-'Arakhin*, Jerusalem, 1982
Leiner, Jacob of Radzhyn, *Bet Ya'akov*, Jerusalem, 1975
Levine, A., *Zikhron Meir*, Toronto, 1985
Lewin, A., Responsa *Avney Ḥefetz*, Munich, 1948
Lewin, B. M. (ed.), *Otzar ha-Geonim, Pesaḥim*, Jerusalem, 1931
Lillie, William, *An Introduction to Ethics*, London, 1948
Lipschitz, Israel, *Tiferet Yisrael*, Commentary to the Mishnah, Vilna, 1911
Loewe, Herbert, 'Judaism', in *ERE*, vol. VII, pp. 581–609
Loewe, Raphael (ed.), *Studies in Rationalism, Judaism and Universalism in Memory of Leon Roth*, London, 1966
Luzzatto, M. H., *Kelaḥ Pitḥey Ḥokhmah*, Jerusalem, 1961
Mesillat Yesharim, trans. into English and ed M. M. Kaplan, *The Path of the Upright*, Philadelphia, 1936
Maimonides, Moses, Commentary to the Mishnah in Romm edn, Vilna, of the Babylonian Talmud and ed. J. Kapah, Jerusalem, 1963
Maamar Teḥiat ha-Metim, Maimonides' Treatise on the Resurrection, ed. Joshua Finkel, New York, 1939
Mishneh Torah (*Yad ha-Ḥazakah*), various editions
Moreh Nevukhim, Lemberg, 1886; English trans. S. Pines, *The Guide of the Perplexed*, Chicago, Ill. 1963
Malter, Henry, *The Treatise Ta'anit of the Babylonian Talmud*, Philadelphia, 1928
Mannaseh, b. Israel, *Sefer Nishmat Ḥayyim*, Stettin, 1851
Markus, A., *ha-Ḥasidut*, Hebrew trans. M. Shenfeld, Tel-Aviv, 1954
Medini, H. H., *Sedey Ḥemed*, ed. A. I. Friedmann, New York, 1962
Meir of Lublin, *Maharam*, Romm edn of the Talmud, Vilna
Meir of Rottenburg, *Teshuvot-Pesakim U-Minhagim*, ed. I. Z. Kahana, Jerusalem, 1957–62
Meiri of Perpignan, Menahem, *Bet ha-Beḥirah, Berakhot*, ed. S. Dickmann, Jerusalem, 1965

Menahem Mendel of Lubavitch, *Derekh Mitzvotekha*, Poltava, 1911
Mendelssohn, Moses, *Phaedon*, English trans. Charles Cullen, London, 1789
Mill, J. S., *On Liberty*, Everyman edn, London, 1924
Moore, George Foot, *History of Religions*, Edinburgh, 1914
Judaism in the First Centuries of the Christian Era, Cambridge, Mass., 1927
Mordecai of Chernobil, *Likkutey Torah*, Lemberg, 1865
Mordecai Joseph of Izbica, *Mey ha-Shiloaḥ*, vol. I, Vienna, 1860, vol. II, Lublin, 1922; photocopy in one vol. Brooklyn and New York, 1973
Munitz, Milton K. (ed.), *A Modern Introduction to Ethics*, Glencoe, Ill., 1958
Nahmanides, Moses, Commentary to the Pentateuch, ed. C. B. Chavel, Jerusalem, 1959
'*Iggeret ha-Kodesh*', Collected Writings of *Ramban*, ed. C. B. Chavel, Jerusalem, 1964, vol. II, pp. 315–37; English trans. Seymour J. Cohen, *The Holy Letter: A Study in Medieval Sexual Morality*, New York, 1976
Neumark, David, *Toledot ha-'Ikkarim be-Yisrael*, Odessa, 1912
Nicholson, R. A., *The Mystics of Islam*, London, 1914
Nissim Gerondi, Commentary to tractate *Nedarim* in the Romm edn, Vilna, of the Babylonian Talmud
Nott, Kathleen, *The Good Want Power: An Essay on the Psychological Possibilities of Liberalism*, London, 1977
Ochs, Peter, 'Individuality', in Arthur A. Cohen and Paul Mendes-Flor (eds.), *Contemporary Jewish Religious Thought*, pp. 483–5
Olson, Robert G., *An Introduction to Existentialism*, New York, 1963
Otto, Rudolph, *Mysticism East and West*, trans. Bertha L. Bracey and Richenda C. Payne, New York, 1957
Outka, Gene, and Reeder, John P. Jnr (eds.), *Religion and Morality*, New York, 1973
Palaggi, Hayyim, *Ḥikkekey Lev*, Salonika, 1840
Perfet, Isaac b. Sheshet, Responsa *Ribash*, photocopy of I. H. Daiches (ed.), New York, 1943
Perkins, Robert L. (ed.), *Kierkegaard's Fear and Trembling: Critical Appraisals*, Birmingham, Ala., 1981
Perry, Ralph Barton, 'The Individual as the Seat of Value', in M. Munitz (ed.), *A Modern Introduction to Ethics*, pp. 474–96
Philo of Alexandria, Works in ten volumes, trans. F. H. Coulson and G. H. Whitaker, Loeb Classical Library, Cambridge, Mass., 1962
Plotzki, Meir Dan, *Keli Ḥemdah*, Pietrikow, 1927
Rashi Commentary of R Shlomo Yitzhaki to Bible and Talmud, various editions
Rivkind, Isaac, 'A Responsum of Leo da Modena on Uncovering the Head' (Heb.), in *Louis Ginzberg Jubilee Volume*, New York, 1945, Hebrew Section, pp. 401–23
Roberts, David E., *Existentialism and Religious Belief*, New York, 1959
Rosenzweig, Franz, *Star of Redemption*, trans. William W. Hallo, London, 1971
Roth, Sol, *Halakhah and Politics: The Jewish Idea of a State*, New York, 1988

Rowley, H. H. (ed.), *The Old Testament and Modern Study*, Oxford, 1956
Rudnik, I., *Sedey Yitzḥak*, London, 1960
Saadia Gaon, *Emunot ve-De'ot*, various editions; English trans. Samuel Rosenblatt, *Beliefs and Opinions*, New Haven, Conn., 1948
Schechter, Solomon, *Studies in Judaism*, Philadelphia, 1945
Scholem, Gershom G., *Kabbalah*, Jerusalem, 1974
Major Trends in Jewish Mysticism, 3rd edn, London, 1955
The Messianic Idea in Judaism, New York, 1971
Seliger, Joseph, Collected Writings (Heb.), ed. Leah Seliger, Jerusalem, 1939
Sevin, S. J., *Likkutey Torah*, Vilna, 1884, photocopy Brooklyn, 1976
le-Or ha-Halakhah, Jerusalem, 1959
Torah Or, Brooklyn, 1955
Sefarim ve-Soferim, Tel-Aviv, 1959
Shulḥan 'Arukh ha-Rav, New York, 1954
Tanya, Vilna, 1930, and various editions
Shohet, D. M., *The Jewish Court in the Middle Ages*, New York, 1931
Simhah of Vitry, *Maḥzor Vitry*, ed. S. Hurwitz and A. Berliner, Nürnberg, 1923
Singer, Simeon, *The Authorised Daily Prayer Book*, London, 1962
Skinner, J., *Genesis* in the International Critical Commentary (ICC), Edinburgh, 1930
Soloveitchik, J. B., *Halakhic Man*, trans. Lawrence Kaplan, Philadelphia, 1983
'The Lonely Man of Faith', *Tradition* 7:2 (Spring, 1978, 5–67
Spira, Hayyim Eleazar, Responsa *Minḥat Eleazar*, Munkacs, 1930
Swami Prabhavananda and Manchester, Frederick, *The Upanishads*, New York, 1957
Taylor, Charles, *Sayings of the Jewish Fathers*, Cambridge, 1900
Teicher, Zevi Elimelech, *Ma'aseh ha-Tzedakah*, Premisla, 1874; photocopy, Jerusalem, 1978
Teitelbaum, M., *ha-Rav mi-Ladi*, Warsaw, 1913
Tishby, I., *Mishnat ha-Zohar*, vol. II, Jerusalem, 1961
Tosafists, Commentaries and Glosses to the Babylonian Talmud, various editions
Travers Herford, R., *Sayings of the Fathers*, New York, 1962
Uceda, Samuel b. Isaac, *Midrash Shemuel*, Venice, 1579
Ullendorff, E., 'Thought Categories in the Hebrew Bible', in Raphael Loewe, *Studies...*, pp. 275–88
Underhill, Evelyn, *Mysticism*, London, 1940
Urbach, E., *Ḥazal*, Jerusalem, 1960
Van der Leeuw, G., *Religion in Essence and Manifestation*, London, 1938
Vital, Hayyim, *'Etz Hayyim*, Koretz, 1784
Sha'arey Kedushah, Sulzbach, 1758
Waldinberg, Eliezer, Responsa *Tzitz Eliezer*, vol. V, Jerusalem, 1957
Wegner, Judith Romney, *Chattel or Person*, New York, 1988

Weingarten, Joab, *Ḥelkat Yoav*, Jerusalem, 1985
Weiss, J. G., 'The Religious Determinism of Joseph Mordecai of Izbica' (Heb.), in S. Ettinger *et al.* (eds.), *The Baer Jubilee Volume*, pp. 447–53
Werblowsky, R. J. Z., *Joseph Karo*, Oxford, 1962
'Philo and the Zohar', in *JJS*, 10 (1959), 38–9
Wiener, M., *Hadrat Panim Zakan*, Brooklyn and New York, 1977
Wolfson, H. A., *Philo*, 2 vols., Cambridge, Mass., 1948
Wolk, Samuel J. B., 'Individualism', in *UJE*, vol. v, pp. 559–63
Yosef Hayyim of Baghdad, Responsa *Rav Pe'alim*, Jerusalem, 1901–12
Zaehner, R. C., *Hindu and Muslim Mysticism*, London, 1960
Mysticism Sacred and Profane, Oxford, 1957
Zeitlin, Hillel, 'Mafteaḥ le-Sefer ha-Zohar', in *ha-Tekufah*, vol. IX, Warsaw, 1921
Zeritzski, David, *Torat ha-Musar*, Tel-Aviv, n.d.
Zevi, Elimelech of Dynow, *Beney Yissakhar*, various editions and Israel, n.p., n.d.
Zinger, J. D., *Ziv ha-Minhagim*, Jerusalem, 1971

Index